HEALTH CARE IN TRANSITION

GEOGRAPHIC VARIATION IN PRIVATE HEALTH CARE SPENDING

SELECTED PROCEDURES AND METROPOLITAN AREAS

HEALTH CARE IN TRANSITION

Additional books in this series can be found on Nova's website under the Series tab.

Additional e-books in this series can be found on Nova's website under the e-book tab.

HEALTH CARE IN TRANSITION

GEOGRAPHIC VARIATION IN PRIVATE HEALTH CARE SPENDING

SELECTED PROCEDURES AND METROPOLITAN AREAS

DERRICK WATKINS
EDITOR

nova publishers
New York

Library of Congress Cataloging-in-Publication Data

ISBN: 978-1-63482-875-8

Published by Nova Science Publishers, Inc. † New York

CONTENTS

PREFACE

This book examines how spending per episode of care for certain high-cost procedures varies across geographic areas for private payers; and how the mix of service types, and the volume, intensity, and price of services contribute to variation in episode spending across geographic areas for private payers.

Chapter 1 – Research shows that spending on health care varies by geographic area and that higher spending in an area is not always associated with better quality of care. While a substantial body of research exists on geographic variation in spending in Medicare, less research has been done on variation in private sector health care spending, although this spending accounts for about a third of overall health care spending. As U.S. health expenditures continue to rise, policymakers and others have expressed interest in better understanding spending variation and how health care systems can operate efficiently—that is, providing equivalent or higher quality care while maintaining or lowering current spending levels.

Chapter 2 – People obtain insurance to protect themselves against the possibility of financial loss in the future. Health insurance provides protection against the possibility of financial loss due to high health care expenses. Also, people do not know ahead of time exactly what their health care expenses will be, so paying for health insurance on a regular basis helps ease their out-of-pocket spending.

While health coverage continues to be mostly a private enterprise in this country, government plays an increasingly significant role. Government has initiated and responded to dynamics in medicine, the economy, and the workplace through legislation and public policies. One of the most recent efforts was enactment and ongoing implementation of the Patient Protection and Affordable Care Act (ACA; P.L. 111-148, as amended). ACA includes provisions to encourage the expansion of health insurance coverage, and establish new federal health insurance standards, among other reforms.

Americans obtain health insurance in different settings and through a variety of methods. In 2013, a majority (64.2%) of Americans obtained health insurance through the private sector, which includes both employer-sponsored and individual market coverage. Public programs (Medicare, Medicaid/CHIP, or health services for military service members and veterans) provided coverage to 34.3% of Americans. Approximately 13.4% of Americans were uninsured for the entire year of 2013.

Health insurance benefits are delivered and financed under different systems. The factors that distinguish one delivery system from another are many, including how health care is financed, how much access to providers and services is controlled, and how much authority the enrollee has to design her/his health plan. To illustrate, managed care is characterized by predetermined restrictions on accessing services and providers, whereas individual decision-making regarding use of health benefits is a hallmark of consumer driven health care, such as health savings accounts. As economic conditions change, a specific delivery system may gain or lose the interest of affected parties.

In: Geographic Variation …
Editor: Derrick Watkins
ISBN: 978-1-63482-875-8

Chapter 1

PRIVATE HEALTH INSURANCE: GEOGRAPHIC VARIATION IN SPENDING FOR CERTAIN HIGH-COST PROCEDURES DRIVEN BY INPATIENT PRICES*

United States Government Accountability Office

WHY GAO DID THIS STUDY

Research shows that spending on health care varies by geographic area and that higher spending in an area is not always associated with better quality of care. While a substantial body of research exists on geographic variation in spending in Medicare, less research has been done on variation in private sector health care spending, although this spending accounts for about a third of overall health care spending. As U.S. health expenditures continue to rise, policymakers and others have expressed interest in better understanding spending variation and how health care systems can operate efficiently—that is, providing equivalent or higher quality care while maintaining or lowering current spending levels.

* This is an edited, reformatted and augmented version of the United States Government Accountability Office publication, GAO-15-214, dated December 2014.

GAO was asked to examine geographic variation in private sector health care spending. GAO examined (1) how spending per episode of care for certain high-cost procedures varies across geographic areas for private payers, and (2) how the mix of service types, and the volume, intensity, and price of services contribute to variation in episode spending across geographic areas for private payers. Using a large private sector claims database for 2009 and 2010, GAO examined spending by MSA for episodes of care for three commonly performed inpatient procedures and examined spending by hospital inpatient, hospital outpatient, postdischarge, professional, and ancillary service categories. For inpatient and professional services, GAO examined the volume, intensity, and price of services. GAO's findings may not be generalizable to all private insurers due to data limitations.

What GAO Found

Spending for an episode of care in the private sector varied across metropolitan statistical areas (MSA) for coronary stent placement, laparoscopic appendectomy, and total hip replacement, even after GAO adjusted for geographic differences in the cost of doing business and differences in enrollee demographics and health status. MSAs in the highest-spending quintile had average adjusted episode spending that was 74 to 94 percent higher than MSAs in the lowest-spending quintile, depending on the procedure. MSAs with higher spending on one procedure generally had higher spending on the other two procedures. High- or low-spending MSAs were not concentrated in particular regions of the nation.

The price of the initial hospital inpatient admission accounted for 91 percent or more of the difference in episode spending between MSAs in the lowest- and highest-spending quintiles. The price of the initial admission was the largest contributor to the difference for two reasons. First, it represented the largest percentage of adjusted episode spending. For example, for total hip replacement, the average price of the initial admission was $17,134, representing 76 percent of the $22,463 in total episode spending for MSAs in the lowest-spending quintile and $30,332, representing 82 percent of the $36,969 in total episode spending for MSAs in the highest-spending quintile. Second, the price of the initial admission varied considerably across MSAs. For MSAs in the highest-spending quintile, the average price of the initial admission for total hip replacement was 77 percent higher than for MSAs in the lowest-spending quintile. Professional services—office visits and other services provided by a physician or other health professional—were the second largest contributor to geographic differences in episode spending, but accounted for 7 percent or less of the difference in episode spending between MSAs in the lowest- and highest-spending quintiles. (See table.) MSAs in the highest-spending quintile had higher average prices and intensity (a measure of the resources needed to provide a service) but fewer services (volume) than MSAs in the lowest-spending quintile for all three procedures.

The Department of Health and Human Services provided technical comments on a draft of this report, which were incorporated as appropriate.

Contributions of Each Service Category to Differences in Average Episode Spending between MSAs in Lowest- and Highest-Spending Quintiles

Service category	Coronary stent placement	Laparoscopic appendectomy	Total hip replacement
Hospital inpatient—Price of initial admission	92%	96%	91%
Hospital inpatient—Readmissions	1%	0%	0%
Hospital outpatient	1%	1%	1%
Postdischarge	0%	0%	0%
Professional	5%	3%	7%
Ancillary and unclassified	1%	0%	1%
Total	**100%**	**100%**	**100%**

Source: GAO analysis of 2009 and 2010 claims data from Truven Health Analytics. | GAO-15-214.

ABBREVIATIONS

GDP	gross domestic product
IOM	Institute of Medicine
MedPAC	Medicare Payment Advisory Commission
MSA	metropolitan statistical area
RVU	relative value unit

***

December 29, 2014

The Honorable Henry A. Waxman
Ranking Member
Committee on Energy and Commerce
House of Representatives

Dear Mr. Waxman:

National health expenditures are projected to grow from $2.8 trillion in 2012 to over $5 trillion in 2023, outpacing gross domestic product (GDP) growth over this period, and accounting for almost 20 percent of GDP by 2023.[1] The United States spends significantly more on health care than any other nation, yet health outcomes in the United States are not necessarily better than those of other nations with lower spending. Further, research on U.S. health care spending has shown that spending can vary by geographic area and that this variation remains even after accounting for important differences across areas, such as differing health status of populations and differing costs of doing business. Studies have also shown that higher spending is not always associated with better quality of care.[2] As U.S. health expenditures continue to rise, there is widespread interest among policymakers and others in improving their understanding of drivers of spending and in learning more about where and how health care systems operate efficiently—that is, provide equivalent or higher quality care while maintaining or lowering current spending levels.

While researchers have developed a substantial body of work on geographic variation in Medicare spending,[3] less research has been done on geographic variation in private sector health care spending. Researchers have primarily focused on Medicare spending because of the availability of Medicare spending data. However, private sector spending on health care accounts for about one-third of U.S. health expenditures and more comprehensive private sector data has become available in recent years.[4] Additional research on private sector spending will provide important contributions to an overall understanding of geographic variation in health care spending.

A useful framework for exploring geographic variation and reasons behind geographic spending differences is examining spending within an episode of care—defined as the care and services provided for a specific medical problem, condition, or illness during a specific time period. Using the episode, we can examine the contribution of components that drive spending variation. These components include the mix of services provided—hospital inpatient, hospital outpatient, physician and other professional services, postdischarge, and ancillary services—and the volume, intensity, and price of those services.[5] A greater understanding of the reasons for higher or lower spending in certain areas may provide insights into the policy options that are most likely to be effective at promoting efficiencies and cost savings.

You asked us to examine geographic variation in private sector health care spending. We examined

- how spending per episode of care for certain high-cost procedures varies across geographic areas for private payers and
- how the mix of service types, and the volume, intensity, and price of services contribute to variation in episode spending across geographic areas for private payers.

To examine how spending per episode of care for certain high-cost procedures varies across geographic areas, we calculated average episode spending by metropolitan statistical areas (MSA).[6] We created episodes based on an inpatient admission for each of the following procedures: coronary stent placement, laparoscopic appendectomy, and total hip replacement.[7] For the years we analyzed in the private sector database—2009 and 2010—these procedures were commonly performed and associated with high levels of national spending.[8] These procedures also represent different medical specialties. In addition, we selected hospital-based procedures because the United States spends more nationally on hospital services than any other type of health care service.[9] To create the episodes, which included all services from the day of admission to 30 days after discharge and certain services in the 3 days prior to admission,[10] we used private sector health insurance claims and enrollment data from the Truven Health Analytics MarketScan® Commercial Claims and Encounters Database for 2009 and 2010. This database contains claims for over 50 million enrollees paid by over 100 private insurers across 50 states and the District of Columbia in 2009 and 2010. We assigned episodes to MSAs based on the location of the hospital inpatient admission, keeping only MSAs that had a sufficient number of episodes to support our analyses.[11] We calculated unadjusted spending by using the payment amounts on the claims. We then adjusted spending for geographic differences in the cost of doing business and differences in the demographics and health status of enrollees in each MSA.[12] Using all MSAs included in our analyses, we determined the distribution of average episode spending for each procedure, and, using the 78 MSAs with a sufficient number of episodes for all three procedures, we calculated the extent to which MSAs with high or low episode spending for one procedure also had high or low episode spending for another procedure.

To examine how the mix of service types, and the volume, intensity, and price of services contribute to variation in episode spending across geographic areas, we calculated and reported on differences in these components for the 78 MSAs with a sufficient number of episodes for all three procedures, focusing on MSAs in the lowest- and highest-spending quintile for each procedure. We analyzed the mix of service types by assigning all spending within an episode to one of five service categories: (1) hospital inpatient, (2) hospital outpatient, (3) postdischarge, (4) professional, and (5) ancillary.[13] For hospital inpatient and professional services, we also examined volume, intensity, and price of services.[14] For hospital inpatient services, we measured volume as the number of days in the hospital stay, and we measured price by the amount spent on the initial hospital inpatient admission (which excluded spending on any subsequent readmissions), because hospitals are generally paid one amount per admission regardless of the patient's length of stay or the services delivered. For professional services, we measured volume as the number of services provided, and we measured intensity by using the relative value unit (RVU), which is an estimate of the resources needed to provide a given service.[15] We calculated the price per unit of intensity by dividing average spending on professional services by the total units of intensity (number of RVUs) associated with those services. See appendix I for a more detailed description of our methodology.

We assessed the reliability of the MarketScan database by reviewing documentation, discussing the database with knowledgeable officials, and performing data reliability checks, and we determined the data were sufficiently reliable for our purposes.

Our study had some limitations. We reported results only for those MSAs in which we had a sufficient number of episodes to ensure the reliability of our results for each procedure, but our results included MSAs that constituted a majority of the U.S. population. Depending on the procedure, 60 to 63 percent of the U.S. population lives in the MSAs included.[16] In addition, although we chose procedures that were commonly performed and associated with high levels of national spending, our results may not be generalizable to other procedures not included in our analysis. Also, while the data used for our analyses were from one of the largest private insurance data sources, the data did not include all private payers and are not necessarily representative of the private health insurance market in the United States. As such, our findings may not be generalizable to this broader private health insurance market. For example, in 2009 and 2010, the percentage of enrollees in the data were disproportionately from large self-insured firms, which tend to have more generous benefit packages compared with other payers, and they were also disproportionately from the South. Finally, 2009 and 2010 data do not reflect the impact of more recent policy or other changes potentially affecting private sector health care spending, such as the implementation of the Patient Protection and Affordable Care Act.

We conducted our work from January 2012 to December 2014 in accordance with all sections of GAO's Quality Assurance Framework that are relevant to our objectives. The framework requires that we plan and perform the engagement to obtain sufficient and appropriate evidence to meet our stated objectives and to discuss any limitations in our work. We believe that the information and data obtained, and the analysis conducted, provide a reasonable basis for any findings and conclusions in this product.

BACKGROUND

Private sector data have become increasingly available to researchers, and several studies have established that significant geographic variation in spending exists in the private sector. For example, in a recent comprehensive assessment of geographic variation in private sector spending, the Institute of Medicine (IOM) reported on the presence of substantial spending variation, concluding that a large amount of the variation remained unexplained after adjusting for enrollee demographic and health status factors, insurance plan factors, and market-level factors, and suggesting that inefficiency is one of the causes of the current levels of variation.[17] Using private sector claims data from two nationwide databases from 2007 through 2009, IOM found unadjusted spending for the area at the 90th percentile was 36 to 42 percent higher than the area at the 10th percentile, depending on the database used.[18] The spending differences existed at all levels of geography IOM studied, including MSAs, and these differences persisted over time. IOM also found that price is a major determinant of geographic variation in the private sector, and estimated that, after adjusting for underlying costs, price accounted for 70 percent of the geographic variation in private sector spending. The researchers attributed the large impact of price in explaining private sector geographic spending variation to the relatively strong market power of providers in some areas.

Other studies, including one by GAO, have reached similar conclusions. The Medicare Payment Advisory Commission (MedPAC) examined geographic variation in private sector spending and estimated that in 2008, hospital inpatient spending for the MSA at the 90th percentile was 90 percent higher than for the MSA at the 10th percentile.[19] MedPAC also found that spending for physician services varied, but less so than hospital inpatient spending. Physician spending at the 90th percentile was 50 percent higher than that at the 10th percentile. Early work by GAO analyzing 2001 private sector claims in the Federal Employees Health Benefits Program also found substantial geographic variation in private sector hospital inpatient prices, physician prices, and spending.[20]

IOM also found that areas with relatively high prices tended to have relatively low utilization and vice versa. In addition, IOM found that private sector utilization varied more for some service types than others. For example, emergency department use was 50 to 100 percent higher for the area at the 90th percentile of utilization relative to the 10th percentile, and hospital outpatient visits were 30 to 46 percent higher. In addition, consistent with other research, use of discretionary services varied substantially. For example, the utilization rate for hip replacement, considered a discretionary procedure, for the area at the 90th percentile was 53 percent higher than the area at the 10th percentile, and other discretionary procedures, such as hysterectomies, lower back surgeries, and nuclear stress tests, had even larger differences.[21]

Researchers from the National Institute for Health Care Reform recently examined geographic variation in spending for hip and knee replacement episodes of care using 2011 claims data for autoworkers and their dependents in nine geographic areas in six states.[22] They defined episodes as those beginning with a hospital admission and including all services up to 30 days postdischarge. Average spending per episode across the nine markets ranged from below $25,000 in Louisville, Kentucky, to above $30,000 in Buffalo, New York.[23] However, variation across the 36 hospitals within these markets varied more than twofold, and all but one of the markets had a lower-spending hospital option, defined as having average episode spending below $25,000. To get a broader measure of variation in episode spending, these researchers also examined all episode types across hospitals.

The spending variations observed for knee and hip replacements held true for other conditions, and hospitals with high spending for one service line (cardiology, orthopedics, etc.) were also likely to have high spending for other service lines. In addition, the price of the initial hospital stay accounted for more than 80 percent of the variation in overall spending. Variation in the prices and volume of physician and other services together accounted for less than one-tenth of the variation in episode spending. These researchers noted that reasons for higher-priced hospitals in some areas included their provision of specialized service lines that other nearby hospitals did not offer, being part of a local hospital system with greater bargaining clout, having unusually good clinical reputations, and being part of a large teaching hospital.

Episode Spending Was 74 to 94 Percent Higher in Highest- Compared with Lowest-Spending Areas, with High- Spending Areas Generally High for All Three Procedures

Episode Spending Was 74 to 94 Percent Higher in the Highest- Compared with Lowest-Spending Areas, Depending on Procedure

We noted variation in episode spending across MSAs for all three procedures, even after adjusting for geographic differences in the cost of doing business and differences in demographics and health status of enrollees in each MSA.

For example, average adjusted episode spending across all MSAs in our analysis for laparoscopic appendectomy was $12,506; however, MSAs in the highest-spending quintile had average adjusted episode spending of $17,047, which was almost 94 percent higher than the average adjusted episode spending of $8,802 for MSAs in the lowest-spending quintile. Average adjusted episode spending for this procedure for individual MSAs ranged from $25,924 in Salinas, California, to $6,166 in Joplin, Missouri. We found similar results for the other two procedures we studied, coronary stent placement and total hip replacement. Average adjusted episode spending for MSAs in the highest-spending quintile was about 84 percent and 74 percent higher than for MSAs in the lowest-spending quintile, respectively. (See figure 1; also, see app. II for complete rankings of MSAs by procedure.) We found greater geographic variation in average episode spending than the research from the National Institute for Health Care Reform, likely because our study included many more geographic areas.[24]

For all three procedures, adjustments to control for geographic differences in the cost of doing business and for differences in demographics and health status of enrollees reduced the extent of variation in spending across MSAs. For example, before adjustment, average episode spending for laparoscopic appendectomy in the highest- spending MSA (Salinas, California) was 511 percent higher than the lowest-spending MSA (Joplin, Missouri); and, after adjustment, spending was 320 percent higher.

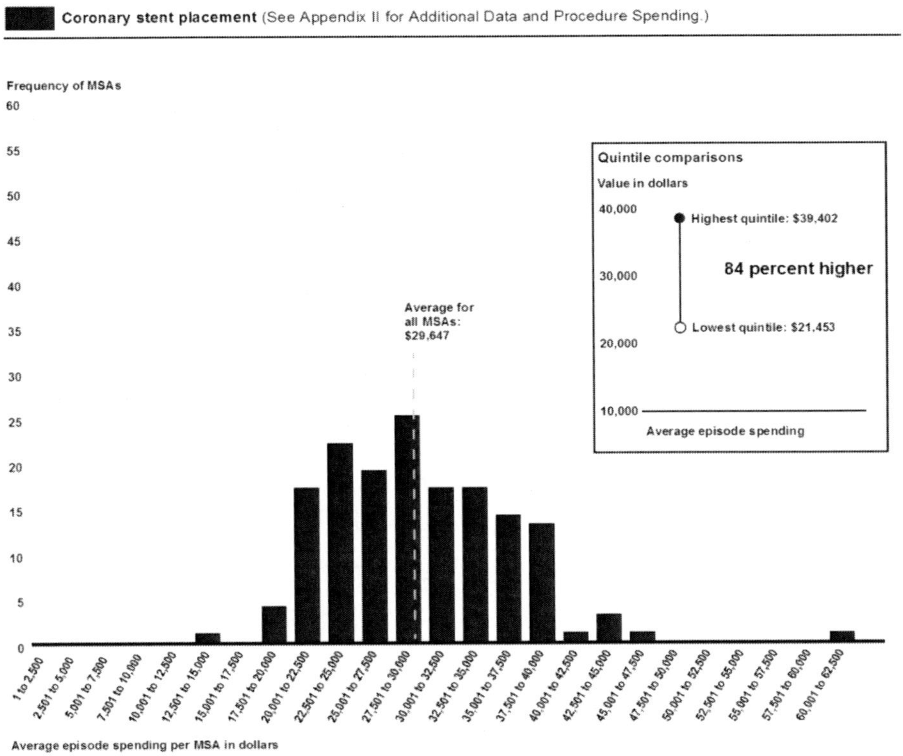

Source: GAO analysis of 2009 and 2010 claims data from Truven Health Analytics. | GAO-15-214.

Note: Data were from 155 MSAs for coronary stent placement episodes, 139 MSAs for laparoscopic appendectomy episodes, and 141 MSAs for total hip replacement episodes. For each procedure, we included all MSAs for which we had a sufficient number of episodes to support our analyses. Spending was adjusted to control for geographic differences in the cost of doing business and differences in demographics and health status of enrollees in each MSA.

Figure 1. Distribution of Average Episode Spending Across Metropolitan Statistical Areas (MSA).

High-Spending Areas Generally Were High- Spending for All Three Procedures

MSAs with higher spending on one procedure generally had higher spending on the other two procedures. For example, Salinas, California, and Fort Wayne, Indiana, were among the highest-spending MSAs for all three procedures, while Hartford, Connecticut, and Youngstown, Ohio, were among the lowest-spending MSAs for all three procedures. We examined average adjusted episode spending in the 78 MSAs that had a sufficient number of episodes for all three procedures and found that the extent of correlation for each pair of procedures for the 78 MSAs ranged from 0.68 to 0.83,[25] consistent with the research from the National Institute for Health Care Reform.[26] (See figure 2)

Despite the overall pattern that MSAs tended to be in the same spending quintiles for all three procedures, there were some exceptions. Notably, Albany, New York, was in the highest-spending quintile for coronary stent placement and total hip replacement but was in the lowest-spending quintile for laparoscopic appendectomy; San Antonio, Texas, was in the highest-spending quintile for total hip replacement but was in the lowest- spending quintile for laparoscopic appendectomy; and Allentown, Pennsylvania, was in the highest-spending quintile for coronary stent placement but was in the lowest-spending quintile for total hip replacement.

We also examined whether high- or low-spending MSAs were concentrated in particular regions of the nation, and we found that they were not.[27] For example, we found 11 MSAs that were in the highest- spending quintile for at least two of the three procedures we examined, and these MSAs were located in different regions of the nation, such as Albany, New York; Fort Wayne, Indiana; Houston, Texas; Madison, Wisconsin; Milwaukee, Wisconsin; Nashville, Tennessee; Salinas, California; and San Diego, California. In addition, some states had MSAs in both the highest- and lowest-spending quintiles for a given procedure. For example, in California, Salinas and San Diego were both in the highest-spending quintile for laparoscopic appendectomy episode spending, whereas Fresno, Oxnard, Riverside, San Jose, and Santa Rosa were all in the lowest-spending quintile. Similarly, in New York, Albany was in the highest-spending quintile for total hip replacement, whereas Rochester was in the lowest-spending quintile.

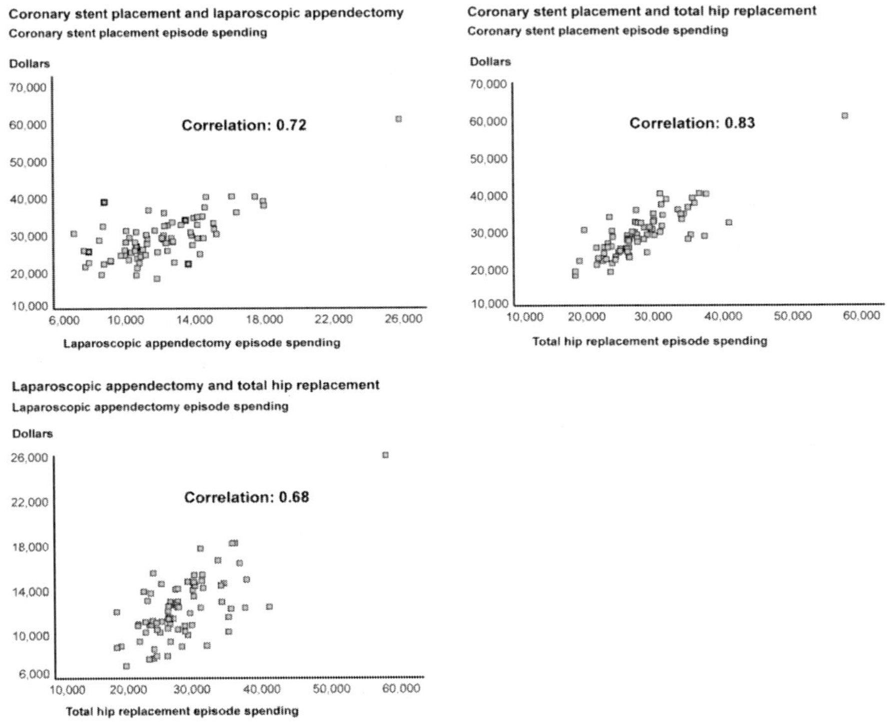

Source: GAO analysis of 2009 and 2010 claims data from Truven Health Analytics. | GAO-15-214.

Note: All correlations shown are significant at p<0.0001. Data were from 78 MSAs. We included all MSAs with a sufficient number of episodes to support our analyses for all three procedures. Spending was adjusted to control for geographic differences in the cost of doing business and differences in demographics and health status of enrollees in each MSA.

Figure 2. Correlation of Average Episode Spending between Procedures.

PRICE PER INITIAL INPATIENT ADMISSION WAS LARGEST CONTRIBUTOR TO GEOGRAPHIC DIFFERENCES IN EPISODE SPENDING

The price of the initial hospital inpatient admission was the largest contributor to differences in private sector episode spending across MSAs.[28] Differences in the price of the initial admission accounted for 91 percent or more of the difference in average adjusted episode spending between the lowest- and highest-spending quintiles. For example, for total hip replacement, the difference in average adjusted episode spending in the MSAs in the lowest- and highest-spending quintiles was $14,506, and $13,198 of that difference— or 91 percent— was attributable to differences in the price of the initial inpatient admission. Similarly, differences in initial inpatient admission prices accounted for 92 and 96 percent of the differences in episode spending between MSAs in the lowest- and highest-spending quintiles for coronary stent placement and laparoscopic appendectomy, respectively (see table 1). The role of inpatient admission price as the primary driver of geographic differences in spending in the private sector has been reported in the literature, such as by the National Institute for Health Care Reform.

Table 1. Contributions of Each Service Category to Differences in Average Episode Spending between Metropolitan Statistical Areas (MSA) in the Lowest- and Highest- Spending Quintiles

Service category	Coronary stent placement	Laparoscopic appendectomy	Total hip replacement
Hospital inpatient—Price of initial admission[a]	92%	96%	91%
Hospital inpatient—Readmissions	1%	0%	0%
Hospital outpatient	1%	1%	1%
Postdischarge	0%	0%	0%
Professional	5%	3%	7%
Ancillary and unclassified	1%	0%	1%
Total	**100%**	**100%**	**100%**

Source: GAO analysis of 2009 and 2010 claims data from Truven Health Analytics. | GAO-15-214.

Note: Data were from 78 MSAs. We included all MSAs with a sufficient number of episodes to support our analyses for all three procedures. For each procedure, the lowest- and highest-spending quintiles each consist of 16 MSAs. Prices and spending were adjusted to control for geographic differences in the cost of doing business and differences in demographics and health status of enrollees in each MSA.

[a] We identified price as the amount spent on the initial hospital inpatient admission (which excluded spending on any subsequent readmissions), because hospitals are generally paid one amount per admission regardless of the patient's length of stay or the services delivered. In addition, measures of intensity for hospital inpatient spending—such as diagnosis-related groups—are assigned based on the patient's clinical condition. Instead, we reported prices adjusted for differences in demographics and health status of enrollees in each MSA.

The price of the initial inpatient admission contributed most to geographic differences in average adjusted episode spending for two reasons. First, the price of the initial admission represented the largest percentage of adjusted episode spending. For the lowest- and highest-spending quintiles in each of the three procedures, at least two-thirds of episode spending was for the price of the hospital inpatient admission. For example, for total hip replacement, the price of the initial admission was $17,134, representing 76 percent of the $22,463 in total episode spending for MSAs in the lowest-spending quintile and $30,332, representing 82 percent of the $36,969 in total episode spending for MSAs in the highest-spending quintile. Second, the average price of the initial inpatient admission varied considerably across MSAs.[29] The difference in the price of the initial inpatient admission in MSAs in the lowest- and highest-spending quintiles ranged from 77 percent to 121 percent, depending on the procedure. For example, for laparoscopic appendectomy, the price of the initial admission was 121 percent higher for MSAs in the highest-spending quintile compared with MSAs in the lowest-spending quintile (see figure 3). Specifically, MSAs in the highest- spending quintile had an average price of $13,177 for the initial admission—and ranged from $11,087 in Colorado Springs, Colorado, to $23,432 in Salinas, California—whereas MSAs in the lowest-spending quintile had an average price of $5,971 for the initial admission—and ranged from $4,528 in Las Vegas, Nevada, to $7,430 in San Antonio, Texas. (See app. IV for average adjusted episode spending by procedure and service category, and app. V for complete rankings of hospital inpatient spending, initial admission price, and number of days by MSA and procedure.)

Although professional services—office visits, hospital consultations, surgeries, and other services provided by a physician or other health professional—were the second largest contributor to geographic differences in average adjusted episode spending, they contributed to a much smaller extent than did the price of the initial inpatient admission. For each of the three procedures, differences in spending on professional services accounted for only 3 to 7 percent of the difference in overall episode spending between MSAs in the lowest- and highest-spending quintiles.

First, professional services contributed a smaller amount to geographic differences in episode spending because they represented a much smaller percentage of episode spending than the price of the initial inpatient admission. For MSAs in the lowest- and highest-spending quintiles in each of the three procedures, 10 to 29 percent of episode spending was for professional services.

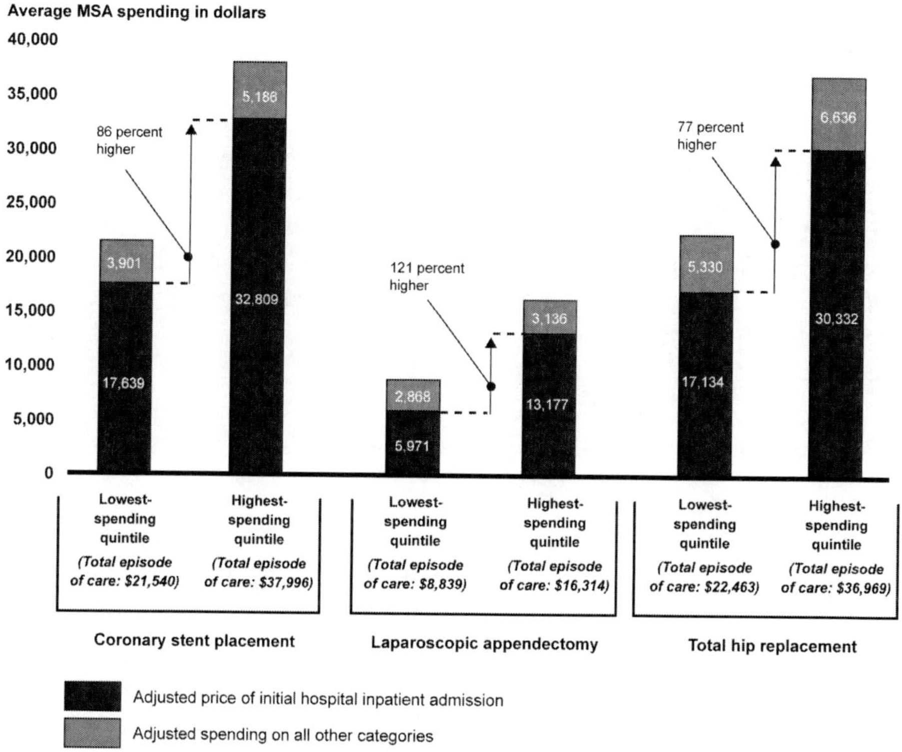

Source: GAO analysis of 2009 and 2010 claims data from Truven Health Analytics. | GAO-15-214.

Note: Data were from 78 MSAs. We included all MSAs with a sufficient number of episodes to support our analyses for all three procedures. For each procedure, the lowest- and highest-spending quintiles each consist of 16 MSAs. Prices and spending were adjusted to control for geographic differences in the cost of doing business and differences in demographics and health status of enrollees in each MSA. Prices and spending may not add to totals because of rounding.

Figure 3. Average Prices of Initial Hospital Inpatient Admissions for Metropolitan Statistical Areas (MSA) in the Lowest- and Highest-Spending Quintiles.

For example, for total hip replacement, spending on professional services was $4,157, representing 19 percent of the $22,463 in total episode spending for MSAs in the lowest-spending quintile and $5,221, representing 14 percent of the $36,969 in total episode spending for MSAs in the highest-spending quintile.

Second, professional services contributed a smaller amount to geographic differences in episode spending because spending on professional services varied less across MSAs. Spending on professional services for MSAs in the highest-spending quintile was between 8 percent and 26 percent higher than in the lowest-spending quintile, depending on the procedure (see figure 4).[30] Overall, spending on professional services ranged widely—for example, from $3,110 in Akron, Ohio, to $9,794 in Madison, Wisconsin, for total hip replacement. (See app. IV for average adjusted episode spending by procedure and service category, and app. VI for complete rankings of professional services spending, number of services, intensity, and price by MSA and procedure.)

Table 2. Professional Services: Difference in Average Spending, Volume, Intensity, and Price

Procedure	Comparison of averages for MSAs in highest- and lowest-spending quintiles			
	Adjusted spending	**Volume (number of services)**	**Intensity**	**Price per unit of intensity**
Coronary stent placement	$791 higher	11.4% lower	4.0% higher	39.8% higher
Laparoscopic appendectomy	$191 higher	12.6% lower	7.3% higher	14.4% higher
Total hip replacement	$1,064 higher	14.8% lower	12.5% higher	33.4% higher

Source: GAO analysis of 2009 and 2010 claims data from Truven Health Analytics. | GAO-15-214.

Note: Data were from 78 MSAs. We included all MSAs with a sufficient number of episodes to support our analyses for all three procedures. For each procedure, the lowest- and highest-spending quintiles each consist of 16 MSAs. Spending, volume, and intensity were adjusted to control for geographic differences in demographics and health status of enrollees in each MSA; spending was also adjusted for differences in the cost of doing business. Intensity is measured by the relative value unit (RVU) assigned to each service.

When we examined how volume, intensity, and prices contributed to differences in spending on professional services, we found that for all three procedures services in MSAs in the highest-spending quintile had higher average prices and higher average intensity than services in MSAs in the lowest-spending quintile, with price having a greater impact than intensity. However, MSAs in the highest-spending quintile used fewer services than MSAs in the lowest-spending quintile, somewhat offsetting the impact of prices on spending. For example, for coronary stent placement, MSAs in the highest-spending quintile had $791 more in spending, 11.4 percent lower volume, 4.0 percent higher intensity, and 39.8 percent higher prices, compared to MSAs in the lowest-spending quintile (see table 2). (See also app. VI for complete rankings of professional services spending, number of services, intensity, and price by MSA and procedure.)

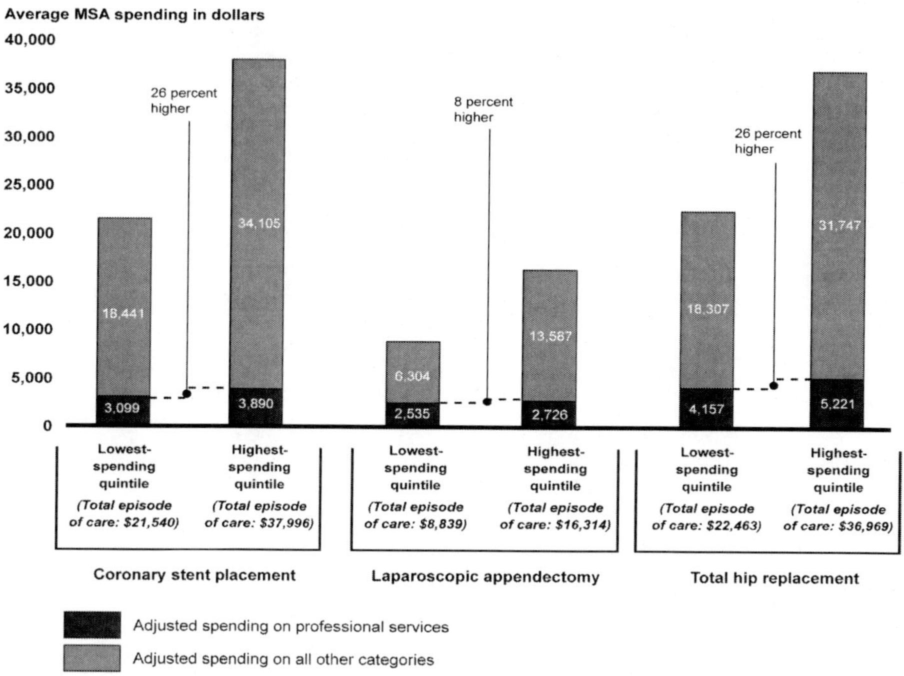

Source: GAO analysis of 2009 and 2010 claims data from Truven Health Analytics. | GAO-15-214.

Note: Data were from 78 MSAs. We included all MSAs with a sufficient number of episodes to support our analyses for all three procedures. For each procedure, the lowest- and highest-spending quintiles each consist of 16 MSAs. Spending was adjusted to control for geographic differences in the cost of doing business and differences in demographics and health status of enrollees in each MSA. Spending may not add to totals because of rounding.

Figure 4. Average Spending on Professional Services in Metropolitan Statistical Areas (MSA) in the Lowest- and Highest-Spending Quintiles.

These findings are consistent with our finding on hospital inpatient spending and with existing research on private sector data, which has generally found that variation in prices drives overall variation in spending across geographic areas. While high-priced areas tend to have lower utilization and vice versa, the variation in prices has a larger effect.

AGENCY COMMENTS

We provided a draft of this product to the Department of Health and Human Services, which did not comment on our findings but provided technical comments. We incorporated these technical comments as appropriate.

Sincerely yours,

James Cosgrove
Director, Health Care

APPENDIX I. DATA AND METHODS

This appendix describes the data and methods we used in our study.

Creating Episodes of Care from Private Health Insurance Claims Data

We created episodes of care based on inpatient admissions for three procedures—coronary stent placement, laparoscopic appendectomy, and total hip replacement[31]—using private health insurance claims and enrollment data from the Truven Health Analytics MarketScan® Commercial Claims and Encounters Database for 2009 and 2010.[32] We identified procedures based on the presence of specific procedure codes in the hospital inpatient and professional service claims.[33]

We selected these procedures because they were commonly performed in the years we analyzed and were associated with high levels of national spending in the MarketScan database.

In addition, we selected procedures that were generally provided by different medical specialties,[34] and we selected hospital-based procedures because the United States spends more nationally on hospital services than any other type of health care service.[35]

We included all services in the episode from the day of admission to 30 days after discharge, and certain services in the 3 days prior to admission. Specifically, we included any outpatient services received by an enrollee in the 3 days prior to admission at the same hospital where the inpatient admission occurred, because those services may be related to the admission. In the episode, we included any drugs provided during the hospital inpatient admission because these drugs were part of the hospital inpatient claims. However, we excluded outpatient drugs, such as prescription drugs, due to limitations of the claims in the MarketScan database.

We excluded enrollees from our study who had inpatient admissions for any of the three procedures outside the 50 states and the District of Columbia, had secondary insurance, or were enrolled in a managed care or other capitated plan.[36] We also excluded enrollees with certain conditions that could increase spending for reasons unrelated to the procedure analyzed. For example, we excluded enrollees who received the procedure more than one time during the episode, enrollees whose overall initial hospital admission was coded as being for a reason unrelated to the procedure analyzed, enrollees with diagnoses of end- stage renal disease, enrollees who were pregnant, and enrollees with a hospice stay.

In addition, we excluded enrollees under the age of 18 for coronary stent placement and total hip replacement episodes, and we excluded enrollees with a diagnosis of appendix rupture for laparoscopic appendectomy episodes.

Analyzing Average Episode Spending across Geographic Areas

We analyzed average episode spending across metropolitan statistical areas (MSA) for each procedure.[37] We assigned episodes to MSAs based on the location of the hospital inpatient admission, and we had a sufficient number of episodes to support our analyses of coronary stent placement in 155 MSAs, laparoscopic appendectomy in 139 MSAs, and total hip replacement in 141 MSAs.[38]

For some analyses where we draw comparisons across procedures, we report data on only the 78 MSAs that had a sufficient number of episodes to support our analyses for all three procedures.

For each procedure, we estimated unadjusted spending and spending adjusted for geographic differences in the cost of doing business and differences in the demographics and health status of enrollees in each MSA. To estimate unadjusted spending, we summed the insurer's allowed payment amount for all services within the episode, including the amount paid by the insurer and any cost-sharing paid by the enrollee.[39] We adjusted for geographic differences in the cost of doing business by using Medicare's payment-adjustment methodology. For services provided by physicians and certain other health professionals, we applied the Geographic Practice Cost Index, which is Medicare's estimate of the geographic differences in the costs of operating a medical practice, to the unadjusted spending for professional services.

For services provided by hospitals, such as during an inpatient admission, and by certain other facilities, we applied the Hospital Wage Index value, which is Medicare's estimate of differences in the wage-related component of the costs of doing business, to a portion of the unadjusted spending for those services.

We additionally adjusted for differences in the demographics and health status of enrollees in each MSA by using a regression-based approach. In the regression, the dependent variable was total cost-adjusted episode spending, and the independent variables were enrollee- level factors (such as age, gender, number of readmissions, and certain comorbidities) and MSA-level indicator variables to identify the portion of the remaining variation in episode spending that was attributable to specific geographic areas.

Using all MSAs in our analyses, we reported the distribution of average adjusted episode spending for each procedure. Using the 78 MSAs with a sufficient number of episodes for all three procedures, we reported the correlation coefficient to show the extent to which MSAs with high or low episode spending for one procedure also had high or low episode spending for another procedure.[40]

We also examined whether MSAs in the lowest- and highest-spending quintile were concentrated in particular regions of the nation.

Analyzing Mix of Service Types

To examine how one of the components of spending—mix of service types—contributes to variation in episode spending across geographic areas, we assigned all adjusted spending within an episode to one of five service categories based on the procedure code for the service and place of service. The five service categories were (1) hospital inpatient, (2) hospital outpatient, (3) postdischarge, (4) professional, and (5) ancillary.[41]

For the 78 MSAs with a sufficient number of episodes for all three procedures, we compared the MSAs in the lowest- and highest-spending quintiles for each procedure, and we reported the extent to which those differences in spending for each service category contributed to differences in episode spending.[42] We also reported the difference in adjusted spending by service category between the quintiles.

Analyzing Volume, Intensity, and Price of Services

To examine how the other components of spending contribute to variation in episode spending for private payers, we analyzed volume, intensity, and price of services for hospital inpatient and professional services.[43]

For hospital inpatient services, we measured volume as the number of days of the hospital stay, and we measured price by the amount of spending on the initial hospital inpatient admission (which excluded spending on any subsequent readmissions) because hospitals are generally paid one amount per admission regardless of the patient's length of stay or the services delivered. In addition, we calculated the extent to which the price of the initial inpatient admission contributed to differences in episode spending between MSAs in the lowest- and highest-spending quintiles.

For professional services, we measured volume as the number of services, measured intensity based on the relative value unit (RVU), which is an estimate of the resources needed to provide a given service,[44] and calculated the price per unit of intensity by dividing average spending on professional services by the total units of intensity (number of RVUs) associated with those services.[45]

Similar to our adjustments for spending, we used a regression-based approach to control for differences in the demographics and health status of enrollees in each MSA. In addition, we compared differences in volume, intensity, and price per unit of intensity between MSAs in the lowest- and highest-spending quintiles.

APPENDIX II: EPISODE SPENDING, BY PROCEDURE, WITHIN METROPOLITAN STATISTICAL AREAS GAO ANALYZED

This appendix ranks metropolitan statistical areas (MSA) by average adjusted episode spending for each of the three procedures we analyzed—coronary stent placement, laparoscopic appendectomy, and total hip replacement.

Table 3. Ranking of Metropolitan Statistical Areas (MSA) by Adjusted Episode Spending for Coronary Stent Placement Episodes

Rank	MSA	Number of episodes	Average adjusted episode spending (in dollars)
1	Salinas, CA	38	60,375
2	Albany, GA	48	45,204
3	[a]	87	44,470
4	[a]	51	43,824
5	Asheville, NC	36	43,578
6	Cape Girardeau-Jackson, MO-IL	42	42,318
7	[a]	62	39,827
8	Charleston, WV	134	39,782
9	San Diego-Carlsbad-San Marcos, CA	80	39,683
10	[a]	77	39,438
11	[a]	165	39,339
12	Rome, GA	59	39,248
13	[a]	28	39,229
14	Milwaukee-Waukesha-West Allis, WI	194	38,596
15	Albany-Schenectady-Troy, NY	27	38,305
16	York-Hanover, PA	56	38,198
17	Mansfield, OH	39	37,808

Rank	MSA	Number of episodes	Average adjusted episode spending (in dollars)
18	Valdosta, GA	26	37,748
19	Lafayette, IN	47	37,612
20	Johnson City, TN	36	37,363
21	[a]	56	37,324
22	Madison, WI	27	37,248
23	[a]	163	36,858
24	[a]	475	36,388
25	Baton Rouge, LA	35	36,327
26	[a]	42	36,222
27	Duluth, MN-WI	34	36,123
28	Houston-Sugar Land-Baytown, TX	634	36,097
29	Winston-Salem, NC	38	36,029
30	[a]	100	35,478
31	Chico, CA	24	35,415
32	Providence-New Bedford-Fall River, RI-MA	70	35,358
33	Parkersburg-Marietta-Vienna, WV-OH	47	35,323
34	Bowling Green, KY	31	34,847
35	Appleton, WI	29	34,614
36	Elkhart-Goshen, IN	53	34,607
37	Green Bay, WI	68	34,539
38	Seattle-Tacoma-Bellevue, WA	237	34,388
39	Fort Wayne, IN	185	34,307
40	Nashville-Davidson-Murfreesboro-Franklin, TN	253	34,258
41	South Bend-Mishawaka, IN-MI	40	34,229
42	Redding, CA	34	34,218
43	[a]	302	33,974
44	Athens-Clarke County, GA	46	33,528
45	Evansville, IN-KY	70	33,510
46	Allentown-Bethlehem-Easton, PA-NJ	244	33,398

Table 3. (Continued)

Rank	MSA	Number of episodes	Average adjusted episode spending (in dollars)
47	Winchester, VA-WV	46	33,041
48	Santa Fe, NM	37	32,920
49	Sacramento-Arden-Arcade-Roseville, CA	86	32,807
50	Orlando-Kissimmee-Sanford, FL	180	32,605
51	Tampa-St. Petersburg-Clearwater, FL	232	32,156
52	Cape Coral-Fort Myers, FL	39	32,143
53	Chattanooga, TN-GA	56	32,134
54	Kansas City, MO-KS	183	32,068
55	Raleigh-Cary, NC	63	31,879
56	Dallas-Fort Worth-Arlington, TX	916	31,847
57	San Jose-Sunnyvale-Santa Clara, CA	43	31,797
58	Lincoln, NE	33	31,748
59	Colorado Springs, CO	51	31,017
60	Syracuse, NY	46	31,008
61	[a]	255	30,680
62	Memphis, TN-MS-AR	114	30,607
63	Niles-Benton Harbor, MI	34	30,341
64	Sherman-Denison, TX	35	30,269
65	[a]	68	30,243
66	[a]	89	30,156
67	Hagerstown-Martinsburg, MD-WV	28	30,013
68	Fresno, CA	62	29,925
69	Grand Rapids-Wyoming, MI	48	29,684
70	Ocala, FL	34	29,547
71	Philadelphia-Camden-Wilmington, PA-NJ-DE-MD	389	29,489
72	Worcester, MA	36	29,427
73	[a]	142	29,393
74	Ann Arbor, MI	67	29,302
75	Bloomington-Normal, IL	40	29,073

Rank	MSA	Number of episodes	Average adjusted episode spending (in dollars)
76	Columbia, MO	43	28,995
77	[a]	54	28,717
78	Denver-Aurora-Broomfield, CO	169	28,698
79	Fayetteville-Springdale-Rogers, AR-MO	49	28,682
80	Chicago-Joliet-Naperville, IL-IN-WI	1,944	28,640
81	New York-Northern New Jersey-Long Island, NY-NJ-PA	1,066	28,629
82	Lakeland-Winter Haven, FL	64	28,607
83	Punta Gorda, FL	31	28,560
84	Portland-Vancouver-Hillsboro, OR-WA	141	28,553
85	Boston-Cambridge-Quincy, MA-NH	331	28,474
86	[a]	192	28,276
87	Decatur, IL	45	28,250
88	Santa Rosa-Petaluma, CA	26	28,065
89	Poughkeepsie-Newburgh-Middletown, NY	24	28,003
90	Muncie, IN	54	27,822
91	Huntington-Ashland, WV-KY-OH	153	27,705
92	Detroit-Warren-Livonia, MI	376	27,544
93	San Antonio-New Braunfels, TX	235	27,489
94	New Orleans-Metairie-Kenner, LA	63	27,480
95	Minneapolis-St. Paul-Bloomington, MN-WI	175	27,308
96	Phoenix-Mesa-Glendale, AZ	263	27,067
97	[a]	66	27,047
98	[a]	673	26,746
99	Oklahoma City, OK	551	26,468
100	[a]	55	26,366
101	[a]	87	26,349
102	Tyler, TX	132	25,953
103	Terre Haute, IN	54	25,896
104	[a]	80	25,813
105	Rochester, NY	83	25,523

Table 3. (Continued)

Rank	MSA	Number of episodes	Average adjusted episode spending (in dollars)
106	Riverside-San Bernardino-Ontario, CA	78	25,322
107	St. Louis, MO-IL	500	25,288
108	Fort Smith, AR-OK	33	25,286
109	Toledo, OH	249	25,210
110	Cincinnati-Middletown, OH-KY-IN	838	25,203
111	Albuquerque, NM	220	25,015
112	Cleveland-Elyria-Mentor, OH	494	24,914
113	Washington-Arlington-Alexandria, DC-VA-MD-WV	210	24,872
114	[a]	27	24,862
115	Shreveport-Bossier City, LA	40	24,848
116	[a]	280	24,753
117	[a]	55	24,682
118	[a]	39	24,456
119	Columbus, OH	450	24,310
120	Tulsa, OK	262	24,088
121	[a]	146	23,938
122	Knoxville, TN	102	23,935
123	Reno-Sparks, NV	47	23,852
124	Naples-Marco Island, FL	32	23,830
125	San Luis Obispo-Paso Robles, CA	37	23,785
126	[a]	32	23,665
127	[a]	203	23,647
128	Bridgeport-Stamford-Norwalk, CT	109	23,135
129	[a]	55	22,848
130	Springfield, MO	48	22,784
131	Los Angeles-Long Beach-Santa Ana, CA	486	22,768
132	Savannah, GA	57	22,585
133	[a]	223	22,570

Rank	MSA	Number of episodes	Average adjusted episode spending (in dollars)
134	Little Rock-North Little Rock-Conway, AR	69	22,439
135	[a]	84	22,391
136	Hartford-West Hartford-East Hartford, CT	353	22,357
137	Columbus, GA-AL	37	22,336
138	Bay City, MI	58	22,236
139	Dayton, OH	174	22,073
140	Oxnard-Thousand Oaks-Ventura, CA	40	22,023
141	[a]	213	21,952
142	Springfield, MA	50	21,937
143	Joplin, MO	60	21,699
144	[a]	1,585	21,664
145	Akron, OH	128	21,664
146	[a]	66	21,651
147	Canton-Massillon, OH	55	21,225
148	Las Vegas-Paradise, NV	115	20,969
149	Lexington-Fayette, KY	196	20,602
150	[a]	332	20,590
151	Youngstown-Warren-Boardman, OH-PA	216	18,829
152	Louisville-Jefferson County, KY-IN	277	18,677
153	Birmingham-Hoover, AL	63	17,768
154	[a]	39	17,710
155	Huntsville, AL	33	14,448

Source: GAO analysis of 2009 and 2010 claims data from Truven Health Analytics. | GAO-15-214.

Note: Data were from 155 MSAs. We included all MSAs with a sufficient number of coronary stent placement episodes to support our analyses. Spending was adjusted to control for geographic differences in the cost of doing business and differences in demographics and health status of enrollees in each MSA.

[a] MSA name withheld to protect the confidentiality of entities that contributed private data.

Table 4. Ranking of Metropolitan Statistical Areas (MSA) by Adjusted Episode Spending for Laparoscopic Appendectomy Episodes

Rank	MSA	Number of episodes	Average adjusted episode spending (in dollars)
1	Salinas, CA	68	25,924
2	Janesville, WI	20	22,677
3	Fort Collins-Loveland, CO	21	21,766
4	Anchorage, AK	20	20,746
5	Reading, PA	50	18,142
6	Madison, WI	32	18,123
7	Milwaukee-Waukesha-West Allis, WI	170	18,096
8	[a]	26	18,085
9	Lynchburg, VA	27	17,745
10	Charleston, WV	33	17,640
11	[a]	34	17,328
12	Port St. Lucie, FL	21	17,104
13	[a]	36	16,588
14	[a]	83	16,323
15	[a]	67	15,724
16	Grand Rapids-Wyoming, MI	30	15,444
17	Colorado Springs, CO	31	15,318
18	Santa Barbara-Santa Maria-Goleta, CA	27	15,307
19	Orlando-Kissimmee-Sanford, FL	215	15,267
20	Farmington, NM	48	15,244
21	[a]	134	15,202
22	[a]	162	15,052
23	San Diego-Carlsbad-San Marcos, CA	174	14,859
24	Pensacola-Ferry Pass-Brent, FL	26	14,835
25	[a]	106	14,761
26	[a]	26	14,704
27	Lakeland-Winter Haven, FL	56	14,678
28	Seattle-Tacoma-Bellevue, WA	349	14,644
29	Fort Wayne, IN	39	14,543

Rank	MSA	Number of episodes	Average adjusted episode spending (in dollars)
30	Columbus, OH	164	14,478
31	Portland-Vancouver-Hillsboro, OR-WA	219	14,337
32	Nashville-Davidson-Murfreesboro-Franklin, TN	72	14,335
33	Cape Coral-Fort Myers, FL	38	14,327
34	Baton Rouge, LA	34	14,149
35	[a]	110	14,115
36	[a]	157	14,042
37	Omaha-Council Bluffs, NE-IA	56	14,017
38	Ann Arbor, MI	100	13,986
39	[a]	42	13,933
40	Kalamazoo-Portage, MI	17	13,926
41	Lima, OH	35	13,851
42	Deltona-Daytona Beach-Ormond Beach, FL	26	13,842
43	Akron, OH	22	13,788
44	Palm Bay-Melbourne-Titusville, FL	18	13,685
45	Allentown-Bethlehem-Easton, PA-NJ	108	13,634
46	Jacksonville, FL	95	13,618
47	Tampa-St. Petersburg-Clearwater, FL	202	13,374
48	El Paso, TX	93	13,229
49	Lawton, OK	22	13,106
50	Modesto, CA	34	13,103
51	[a]	57	13,063
52	[a]	20	13,004
53	Dayton, OH	49	12,973
54	Huntington-Ashland, WV-KY-OH	60	12,897
55	Detroit-Warren-Livonia, MI	198	12,879
56	Sacramento-Arden-Arcade-Roseville, CA	153	12,862
57	Chicago-Joliet-Naperville, IL-IN-WI	1,398	12,800
58	Salt Lake City, UT	44	12,655
59	Kansas City, MO-KS	99	12,596

Table 4. (Continued)

Rank	MSA	Number of episodes	Average adjusted episode spending (in dollars)
60	Sioux City, IA-NE-SD	27	12,572
61	Cincinnati-Middletown, OH-KY-IN	446	12,571
62	Minneapolis-St. Paul-Bloomington, MN-WI	120	12,477
63	Dallas-Fort Worth-Arlington, TX	1,033	12,413
64	Raleigh-Cary, NC	42	12,403
65	Providence-New Bedford-Fall River, RI-MA	103	12,394
66	[a]	41	12,364
67	[a]	67	12,358
68	[a]	23	12,350
69	[a]	197	12,336
70	New York-Northern New Jersey-Long Island, NY-NJ-PA	1,711	12,252
71	Spokane, WA	17	12,161
72	[a]	20	12,088
73	Shreveport-Bossier City, LA	31	12,011
74	Miami-Fort Lauderdale-Pompano Beach, FL	562	11,985
75	Birmingham-Hoover, AL	64	11,960
76	[a]	67	11,865
77	[a]	84	11,851
78	[a]	122	11,851
79	[a]	42	11,840
80	Boulder, CO	22	11,715
81	Atlanta-Sandy Springs-Marietta, GA	309	11,523
82	Bloomington-Normal, IL	19	11,498
83	Houston-Sugar Land-Baytown, TX	722	11,496
84	[a]	24	11,478
85	Boston-Cambridge-Quincy, MA-NH	384	11,417
86	Phoenix-Mesa-Glendale, AZ	554	11,403

Rank	MSA	Number of episodes	Average adjusted episode spending (in dollars)
87	Philadelphia-Camden-Wilmington, PA-NJ-DE-MD	440	11,351
88	Tulsa, OK	143	11,314
89	Rochester, NY	32	11,144
90	Cleveland-Elyria-Mentor, OH	122	11,078
91	[a]	80	11,037
92	Springfield, MA	68	10,958
93	Mobile, AL	22	10,957
94	Stockton, CA	26	10,920
95	Lexington-Fayette, KY	59	10,831
96	Bridgeport-Stamford-Norwalk, CT	154	10,821
97	Springfield, OH	30	10,804
98	[a]	52	10,775
99	Louisville-Jefferson County, KY-IN	90	10,771
100	[a]	38	10,766
101	New Orleans-Metairie-Kenner, LA	65	10,695
102	Toledo, OH	89	10,693
103	Madera-Chowchilla, CA	24	10,579
104	[a]	32	10,555
105	Waco, TX	52	10,505
106	[a]	209	10,470
107	Virginia Beach-Norfolk-Newport News, VA-NC	81	10,458
108	[a]	52	10,393
109	Denver-Aurora-Broomfield, CO	99	10,372
110	Los Angeles-Long Beach-Santa Ana, CA	941	10,351
111	Poughkeepsie-Newburgh-Middletown, NY	105	10,227
112	Memphis, TN-MS-AR	60	10,191
113	San Antonio-New Braunfels, TX	238	10,163
114	[a]	60	10,116
115	Riverside-San Bernardino-Ontario, CA	95	10,108
116	Sherman-Denison, TX	23	9,889

Table 4. (Continued)

Rank	MSA	Number of episodes	Average adjusted episode spending (in dollars)
117	Knoxville, TN	29	9,887
118	Santa Cruz-Watsonville, CA	50	9,789
119	San Luis Obispo-Paso Robles, CA	44	9,584
120	Hartford-West Hartford-East Hartford, CT	354	9,304
121	Syracuse, NY	17	9,285
122	Savannah, GA	44	9,281
123	[a]	55	9,136
124	Chico, CA	23	8,939
125	Albany-Schenectady-Troy, NY	72	8,922
126	[a]	1,122	8,880
127	San Jose-Sunnyvale-Santa Clara, CA	115	8,848
128	Tucson, AZ	84	8,776
129	Youngstown-Warren-Boardman, OH-PA	53	8,747
130	Santa Rosa-Petaluma, CA	19	8,618
131	[a]	52	8,512
132	Lafayette, LA	24	8,042
133	Oxnard-Thousand Oaks-Ventura, CA	64	7,993
134	Albuquerque, NM	276	7,989
135	Las Vegas-Paradise, NV	179	7,773
136	St. Louis, MO-IL	325	7,698
137	Fresno, CA	33	7,096
138	Trenton-Ewing, NJ	34	6,731
139	Joplin, MO	33	6,166

Source: GAO analysis of 2009 and 2010 claims data from Truven Health Analytics. | GAO-15-214.

Note: Data were from 139 MSAs. We included all MSAs with a sufficient number of laparoscopic appendectomy episodes to support our analyses. Spending was adjusted to control for geographic differences in the cost of doing business and differences in demographics and health status of enrollees in each MSA.

[a] MSA name withheld to protect the confidentiality of entities that contributed private data.

Table 5. Ranking of Metropolitan Statistical Areas (MSA) by Adjusted Episode Spending for Total Hip Replacement Episodes

Rank	MSA	Number of episodes	Average adjusted episode spending (in dollars)
1	Salinas, CA	38	57,990
2	Anchorage, AK	30	54,738
3	Albany, GA	27	49,874
4	[a]	49	45,491
5	Santa Barbara-Santa Maria-Goleta, CA	34	42,976
6	Michigan City-La Porte, IN	29	41,377
7	Dallas-Fort Worth-Arlington, TX	954	41,129
8	[a]	35	38,417
9	San Diego-Carlsbad-San Marcos, CA	102	37,906
10	[a]	262	37,669
11	Wausau, WI	30	37,266
12	[a]	65	36,936
13	Madison, WI	26	36,258
14	Lancaster, PA	106	36,049
15	Milwaukee-Waukesha-West Allis, WI	272	35,963
16	[a]	47	35,957
17	New York-Northern New Jersey-Long Island, NY-NJ-PA	1,198	35,682
18	[a]	49	35,421
19	Houston-Sugar Land-Baytown, TX	603	35,332
20	San Antonio-New Braunfels, TX	189	35,319
21	[a]	53	34,965
22	[a]	296	34,856
23	Fort Wayne, IN	147	34,711
24	Sacramento-Arden-Arcade-Roseville, CA	128	34,420
25	Nashville-Davidson-Murfreesboro- Franklin, TN	196	34,311
26	[a]	96	33,944
27	[a]	50	33,899

Table 5. (Continued)

Rank	MSA	Number of episodes	Average adjusted episode spending (in dollars)
28	Elkhart-Goshen, IN	36	33,512
29	Reading, PA	85	33,497
30	South Bend-Mishawaka, IN-MI	73	33,235
31	Salt Lake City, UT	43	33,057
32	Jacksonville, FL	136	32,471
33	Green Bay, WI	75	32,395
34	Albany-Schenectady-Troy, NY	85	32,246
35	Santa Fe, NM	35	32,035
36	Macon, GA	34	31,877
37	[a]	166	31,726
38	Colorado Springs, CO	71	31,648
39	[a]	154	31,550
40	[a]	27	31,429
41	Charleston, WV	68	31,376
42	[a]	53	31,371
43	Spokane, WA	34	31,076
44	Boulder, CO	31	30,958
45	Portland-Vancouver-Hillsboro, OR-WA	217	30,535
46	Orlando-Kissimmee-Sanford, FL	153	30,473
47	Athens-Clarke County, GA	57	30,424
48	Cape Coral-Fort Myers, FL	67	30,422
49	Seattle-Tacoma-Bellevue, WA	405	30,398
50	Tampa-St. Petersburg-Clearwater, FL	173	30,380
51	Springfield, MO	27	30,335
52	Evansville, IN-KY	68	30,323
53	[a]	88	30,205
54	Ocala, FL	39	30,106
55	[a]	54	30,072
56	Lima, OH	33	30,003
57	[a]	168	29,817

Rank	MSA	Number of episodes	Average adjusted episode spending (in dollars)
58	[a]	29	29,692
59	Lakeland-Winter Haven, FL	39	29,480
60	Knoxville, TN	84	29,470
61	Greensboro-High Point, NC	42	29,389
62	Memphis, TN-MS-AR	87	29,073
63	New Orleans-Metairie-Kenner, LA	41	29,035
64	El Paso, TX	52	29,019
65	Atlanta-Sandy Springs-Marietta, GA	863	28,927
66	Asheville, NC	30	28,827
67	Appleton, WI	30	28,648
68	San Jose-Sunnyvale-Santa Clara, CA	88	28,626
69	Oklahoma City, OK	295	28,597
70	Raleigh-Cary, NC	80	28,162
71	Davenport-Moline-Rock Island, IA-IL	67	28,098
72	[a]	470	28,090
73	Huntington-Ashland, WV-KY-OH	73	28,065
74	Denver-Aurora-Broomfield, CO	252	28,042
75	Providence-New Bedford-Fall River, RI-MA	86	27,936
76	[a]	53	27,898
77	Chicago-Joliet-Naperville, IL-IN-WI	1,965	27,774
78	Kansas City, MO-KS	197	27,770
79	Anderson, IN	25	27,753
80	Binghamton, NY	24	27,721
81	Ann Arbor, MI	104	27,709
82	Miami-Fort Lauderdale-Pompano Beach, FL	228	27,551
83	[a]	42	27,450
84	Philadelphia-Camden-Wilmington, PA-NJ-DE-MD	533	27,354
85	[a]	81	27,349
86	Detroit-Warren-Livonia, MI	484	26,945
87	Savannah, GA	114	26,937
88	Cincinnati-Middletown, OH-KY-IN	549	26,868

Table 5. (Continued)

Rank	MSA	Number of episodes	Average adjusted episode spending (in dollars)
89	Bridgeport-Stamford-Norwalk, CT	153	26,858
90	Phoenix-Mesa-Glendale, AZ	274	26,856
91	Tulsa, OK	121	26,651
92	Minneapolis-St. Paul-Bloomington, MN-WI	186	26,628
93	Boston-Cambridge-Quincy, MA-NH	642	26,618
94	Shreveport-Bossier City, LA	31	26,580
95	[a]	304	26,557
96	Albuquerque, NM	234	26,481
97	Wichita, KS	46	26,355
98	Peoria, IL	89	26,320
99	Durham-Chapel Hill, NC	31	26,254
100	North Port-Bradenton-Sarasota, FL	48	26,075
101	Cleveland-Elyria-Mentor, OH	561	25,683
102	Columbus, OH	442	25,627
103	Kalamazoo-Portage, MI	27	25,413
104	[a]	107	25,409
105	Worcester, MA	44	25,125
106	Los Angeles-Long Beach-Santa Ana, CA	711	24,972
107	Springfield, MA	49	24,914
108	Oxnard-Thousand Oaks-Ventura, CA	60	24,908
109	Naples-Marco Island, FL	27	24,878
110	Santa Rosa-Petaluma, CA	36	24,548
111	Modesto, CA	31	24,539
112	Las Vegas-Paradise, NV	113	24,490
113	Grand Rapids-Wyoming, MI	62	24,475
114	Rochester, NY	90	24,365
115	Louisville-Jefferson County, KY-IN	213	24,199
116	Redding, CA	29	24,169
117	Allentown-Bethlehem-Easton, PA-NJ	215	24,117

Rank	**MSA**	**Number of episodes**	**Average adjusted episode spending (in dollars)**
118	[a]	55	23,894
119	St. Louis, MO-IL	434	23,816
120	Dayton, OH	181	23,614
121	Riverside-San Bernardino-Ontario, CA	84	23,361
122	[a]	77	23,348
123	[a]	243	23,314
124	Akron, OH	69	23,100
125	Tucson, AZ	47	23,076
126	Hartford-West Hartford-East Hartford, CT	392	22,478
127	Saginaw-Saginaw Township North, MI	40	22,396
128	Lexington-Fayette, KY	87	22,274
129	Toledo, OH	158	22,242
130	Columbus, GA-AL	55	22,224
131	[a]	80	21,834
132	Reno-Sparks, NV	68	21,718
133	Fresno, CA	82	20,508
134	[a]	1,406	19,794
135	Huntsville, AL	39	19,758
136	Tyler, TX	90	19,731
137	[a]	65	19,518
138	Canton-Massillon, OH	36	19,300
139	[a]	104	19,240
140	Birmingham-Hoover, AL	74	19,166
141	Youngstown-Warren-Boardman, OH-PA	132	19,164

Source: GAO analysis of 2009 and 2010 claims data from Truven Health Analytics. | GAO-15-214.

Note: Data were from 141 MSAs. We included all MSAs with a sufficient number of total hip replacement episodes to support our analyses. Spending was adjusted to control for geographic differences in the cost of doing business and differences in demographics and health status of enrollees in each MSA.

[a] MSA name withheld to protect the confidentiality of entities that contributed private data.

Appendix III. Distribution of Episode Spending

Range of average adjusted episode spending (in dollars)	Number of metropolitan statistical areas (MSA)		
	Coronary stent placement	Laparoscopic appendectomy	Total hip replacement
1 to 2,500	0	0	0
2,501 to 5,000	0	0	0
5,001 to 7,500	0	3	0
7,501 to 10,000	0	21	0
10,001 to 12,500	0	54	0
12,501 to 15,000	1	39	0
15,001 to 17,500	0	12	0
17,501 to 20,000	4	6	8
20,001 to 22,500	17	2	8
22,501 to 25,000	22	1	20
25,001 to 27,500	19	1	23
27,501 to 30,000	25	0	26
30,001 to 32,500	17	0	25
32,501 to 35,000	17	0	11
35,001 to 37,500	14	0	10
37,501 to 40,000	13	0	3
40,001 to 42,500	1	0	2
42,501 to 45,000	3	0	1
45,001 to 47,500	1	0	1
47,501 to 50,000	0	0	1
50,001 to 52,500	0	0	0
52,501 to 55,000	0	0	1
55,001 to 57,500	0	0	0
57,501 to 60,000	0	0	1
60,001 to 62,500	1	0	0
Total	**155**	**139**	**141**

Source: GAO analysis of 2009 and 2010 claims data from Truven Health Analytics. | GAO-15-214.

Note: Data were from 155 MSAs for coronary stent placement episodes, 139 MSAs for laparoscopic appendectomy episodes, and 141 MSAs for total hip replacement episodes. For each procedure, we included all MSAs with a sufficient number of episodes to support our analyses.

Spending was adjusted to control for geographic differences in the cost of doing business and differences in demographics and health status of enrollees in each MSA.

APPENDIX IV. EPISODE SPENDING, BY PROCEDURE, FOR METROPOLITAN STATISTICAL AREAS IN LOWEST- AND HIGHEST-SPENDING QUINTILES

This appendix presents average adjusted episode spending for each of the three procedures we analyzed—coronary stent placement, laparoscopic appendectomy, and total hip replacement—by service category for metropolitan statistical areas (MSA) in the lowest- and highest-spending quintiles.

Table 6. Average Adjusted Episode Spending for Coronary Stent Placement, Metropolitan Statistical Areas (MSA) in Lowest- and Highest-Spending Quintiles

Service category	Lowest-spending quintile (in dollars)	Highest-spending quintile (in dollars)	Comparison
Hospital inpatient	17,908	33,297	86% higher
Hospital outpatient	353	537	52% higher
Postdischarge	15	13	13% lower
Professional	3,099	3,890	26% higher
Ancillary and unclassified	165	258	56% higher
Total, episode of care	**21,540**	**37,996**	**76% higher**

Source: GAO analysis of 2009 and 2010 claims data from Truven Health Analytics. | GAO-15-214.

Note: Data were from 78 MSAs. We included all MSAs with a sufficient number of episodes to support our analyses for all three procedures. The lowest- and highest-spending quintiles each consist of 16 MSAs. Spending was adjusted to control for geographic differences in the cost of doing business and differences in demographics and health status of enrollees in each MSA. Spending may not add to totals because of rounding.

Table 7. Average Adjusted Episode Spending for Laparoscopic Appendectomy, Metropolitan Statistical Areas (MSA) in Lowest- and Highest-Spending Quintiles

Service category	Lowest-spending quintile (in dollars)	Highest-spending quintile (in dollars)	Comparison
Hospital inpatient	6,113	13,331	118% higher
Hospital outpatient	97	159	64% higher
Postdischarge	9	14	56% higher
Professional	2,535	2,726	8% higher
Ancillary and unclassified	85	83	2% lower
Total, episode of care	**8,839**	**16,314**	**85% higher**

Source: GAO analysis of 2009 and 2010 claims data from Truven Health Analytics. | GAO-15-214.

Note: Data were from 78 MSAs. We included all MSAs with a sufficient number of episodes to support our analyses for all three procedures. The lowest- and highest-spending quintiles each consist of 16 MSAs. Spending was adjusted to control for geographic differences in the cost of doing business and differences in demographics and health status of enrollees in each MSA. Spending may not add to totals because of rounding.

Table 8. Average Adjusted Episode Spending for Total Hip Replacement, Metropolitan Statistical Areas (MSA) in Lowest- and Highest-Spending Quintiles

Service category	Lowest-spending quintile (in dollars)	Highest-spending quintile (in dollars)	Comparison
Hospital inpatient	17,323	30,570	76% higher
Hospital outpatient	113	186	65% higher
Postdischarge	673	700	4% higher
Professional	4,157	5,221	26% higher
Ancillary and unclassified	199	291	46% higher
Total, episode of care	**22,463**	**36,969**	**65% higher**

Source: GAO analysis of 2009 and 2010 claims data from Truven Health Analytics. | GAO-15-214.

Note: Data were from 78 MSAs. We included all MSAs with a sufficient number of episodes to support our analyses for all three procedures. The lowest- and highest-spending quintiles each consist of 16 MSAs. Spending was adjusted to control for geographic differences in the cost of doing business and differences in demographics and health status of enrollees in each MSA. Spending may not add to totals because of rounding.

APPENDIX V. HOSPITAL INPATIENT SPENDING AND OTHER INFORMATION, BY METROPOLITAN STATISTICAL AREA AND PROCEDURE

This appendix presents hospital inpatient spending, initial admission price, and number of days, by metropolitan statistical area (MSA), for each of the three procedures we analyzed—coronary stent placement, laparoscopic appendectomy, and total hip replacement.

Table 9. Hospital Inpatient Spending, Initial Admission Price, and Number of Days, by Metropolitan Statistical Area (MSA), for Coronary Stent Placement Episodes

Rank	MSA	Average adjusted spending (in dollars)		Average for initial admission	
		Episode	Hospital inpatient services	Price (in dollars)	Days
1	Salinas, CA[a]	60,375	54,802	54,012	2.55
2	[a,b]	39,827	36,068	35,345	2.98
3	Charleston, WV[a]	39,782	35,589	34,940	2.66
4	San Diego-Carlsbad-San Marcos, CA[a]	39,683	34,709	34,032	1.93
5	Milwaukee-Waukesha-West Allis, WI[a]	38,596	31,550	31,273	2.02
6	Albany-Schenectady-Troy, NY[a]	38,305	34,776	34,580	2.67
7	Madison, WI[a]	37,248	27,109	26,731	1.67
8	[a,b]	36,858	32,864	32,537	2.38

Table 9. (Continued)

Rank	MSA	Average adjusted spending (in dollars)		Average for initial admission	
		Episode	Hospital inpatient services	Price (in dollars)	Days
9	Houston-Sugar Land-Baytown, TX[a]	36,097	31,711	31,291	2.87
10	[a,b]	35,478	31,442	30,861	1.95
11	Providence-New Bedford-Fall River, RI-MA[a]	35,358	31,528	31,329	2.53
12	Seattle-Tacoma-Bellevue, WA[a]	34,388	30,169	29,391	2.19
13	Fort Wayne, IN[a]	34,307	30,059	29,655	2.13
14	Nashville-Davidson-Murfreesboro-Franklin, TN[a]	34,258	29,953	29,609	2.18
15	[a,b]	33,974	30,930	30,422	1.84
16	Allentown-Bethlehem-Easton, PA-NJ[a]	33,398	29,498	28,942	2.35
17	Sacramento-Arden-Arcade-Roseville, CA	32,807	28,396	28,232	1.91
18	Orlando-Kissimmee-Sanford, FL	32,605	29,032	28,711	2.37
19	Tampa-St. Petersburg-Clearwater, FL	32,156	28,796	28,488	2.21
20	Cape Coral-Fort Myers, FL	32,143	28,148	27,765	2.31
21	Kansas City, MO-KS	32,068	27,927	27,182	2.19
22	Raleigh-Cary, NC	31,879	27,839	27,612	2.62
23	Dallas-Fort Worth-Arlington, TX	31,847	28,020	27,729	2.47
24	San Jose-Sunnyvale-Santa Clara, CA	31,797	26,527	25,914	2.23
25	Colorado Springs, CO	31,017	27,341	26,959	1.88
26	[b]	30,680	26,833	26,425	2.28
27	Memphis, TN-MS-AR	30,607	25,683	25,308	2.39
28	[b]	30,243	26,522	26,355	2.16
29	[b]	30,156	23,922	23,796	2.36
30	Fresno, CA	29,925	26,998	26,704	1.73

Rank	MSA	Average adjusted spending (in dollars)		Average for initial admission	
		Episode	Hospital inpatient services	Price (in dollars)	Days
31	Grand Rapids-Wyoming, MI	29,684	26,069	25,874	2.10
32	Philadelphia-Camden-Wilmington, PA-NJ-DE-MD	29,489	25,999	25,227	2.14
33	[b]	29,393	25,436	24,863	2.62
34	Ann Arbor, MI	29,302	25,518	25,033	2.39
35	Denver-Aurora-Broomfield, CO	28,698	24,578	24,085	2.36
36	Chicago-Joliet-Naperville, IL-IN-WI	28,640	24,452	24,048	2.30
37	New York-Northern New Jersey-Long Island, NY-NJ-PA	28,629	24,931	24,515	1.97
38	Lakeland-Winter Haven, FL	28,607	24,567	23,940	2.56
39	Portland-Vancouver-Hillsboro, OR-WA	28,553	23,916	23,726	2.06
40	Boston-Cambridge-Quincy, MA-NH	28,474	24,025	23,662	2.40
41	[b]	28,276	24,273	23,869	2.51
42	Santa Rosa-Petaluma, CA	28,065	23,103	22,956	2.08
43	Huntington-Ashland, WV-KY-OH	27,705	24,019	23,766	3.00
44	Detroit-Warren-Livonia, MI	27,544	24,443	23,744	2.48
45	San Antonio-New Braunfels, TX	27,489	24,032	23,618	2.45
46	New Orleans-Metairie-Kenner, LA	27,480	23,568	23,074	2.40
47	Minneapolis-St. Paul-Bloomington, MN-WI	27,308	21,497	21,057	1.98
48	Phoenix-Mesa-Glendale, AZ	27,067	22,739	22,222	2.05
49	[b]	26,746	22,779	22,545	2.16

Table 9. (Continued)

Rank	MSA	Average adjusted spending (in dollars)		Average for initial admission	
		Episode	Hospital inpatient services	Price (in dollars)	Days
50	[b]	26,349	22,732	21,887	2.85
51	Rochester, NY	25,523	22,354	22,015	1.96
52	Riverside-San Bernardino-Ontario, CA	25,322	21,342	20,944	2.37
53	St. Louis, MO-IL	25,288	21,714	21,294	2.39
54	Toledo, OH	25,210	21,601	21,371	2.34
55	Cincinnati-Middletown, OH-KY-IN	25,203	21,875	21,471	2.19
56	Albuquerque, NM	25,015	21,232	20,794	2.40
57	Cleveland-Elyria-Mentor, OH	24,914	21,232	20,836	2.35
58	Shreveport-Bossier City, LA	24,848	18,990	18,805	2.55
59	[b]	24,753	20,678	20,124	1.79
60	Columbus, OH	24,310	21,266	20,767	2.21
61	Tulsa, OK	24,088	20,619	20,108	2.45
62	[b]	23,938	19,648	19,401	2.23
63	Knoxville, TN[c]	23,935	19,013	18,768	2.43
64	[b,c]	23,647	20,084	19,776	2.43
65	Bridgeport-Stamford-Norwalk, CT[c]	23,135	19,218	18,995	2.18
66	Los Angeles-Long Beach-Santa Ana, CA[c]	22,768	19,135	18,815	1.98
67	Savannah, GA[c]	22,585	18,596	18,596	2.19
68	Hartford-West Hartford-East Hartford, CT[c]	22,357	18,511	18,279	2.27
69	Dayton, OH[c]	22,073	18,839	18,504	2.55
70	Oxnard-Thousand Oaks-Ventura, CA[c]	22,023	18,290	18,290	1.60
71	Springfield, MA[c]	21,937	17,580	17,159	2.96
72	[b,c]	21,664	18,528	18,233	2.32

Rank	MSA	Average adjusted spending (in dollars)		Average for initial admission	
		Episode	Hospital inpatient services	Price (in dollars)	Days
73	Akron, OH[c]	21,664	18,627	18,327	2.25
74	Las Vegas-Paradise, NV[c]	20,969	17,618	17,278	2.65
75	Lexington-Fayette, KY[c]	20,602	18,089	17,824	1.75
76	Youngstown-Warren-Boardman, OH-PA[c]	18,829	15,758	15,420	2.41
77	Louisville-Jefferson County, KY-IN[c]	18,677	15,706	15,447	2.66
78	Birmingham-Hoover, AL[c]	17,768	12,939	12,519	2.41

Source: GAO analysis of 2009 and 2010 claims data from Truven Health Analytics. | GAO-15-214.

Note: Data were from 78 MSAs. We included all MSAs with a sufficient number of episodes to support our analyses for all three procedures. Spending and prices were adjusted to control for geographic differences in the cost of doing business and differences in demographics and health status of enrollees in each MSA.

[a] MSA was in the highest-spending quintile. The 16 MSAs in the highest-spending quintile had an average of $33,297 in spending on hospital inpatient services.

[b] MSA name withheld to protect the confidentiality of entities that contributed private data.

[c] MSA was in the lowest-spending quintile. The 16 MSAs in the lowest-spending quintile had an average of $17,908 in spending on hospital inpatient services.

Table 10. Hospital Inpatient Spending, Initial Admission Price, and Number of Days, by Metropolitan Statistical Area (MSA), for Laparoscopic Appendectomy Episodes

Rank	MSA	Average adjusted spending (in dollars)		Average for initial admission	
		Episode	Hospital inpatient services	Price (in dollars)	Days
1	Salinas, CA[a]	25,924	23,432	23,432	1.56
2	Madison, WI[a]	18,123	13,671	13,480	1.22
3	Milwaukee-Waukesha-West Allis, WI[a]	18,096	14,070	13,873	1.44

Table 10. (Continued)

Rank	MSA	Average adjusted spending (in dollars)		Average for initial admission	
		Episode	Hospital inpatient services	Price (in dollars)	Days
4	Charleston, WV[a]	17,640	14,924	14,673	1.76
5	[a,b]	16,588	13,745	13,337	1.44
6	[a,b]	16,323	14,070	13,984	1.58
7	Grand Rapids-Wyoming, MI[a]	15,444	13,283	13,067	1.33
8	Colorado Springs, CO[a]	15,318	11,087	11,087	1.90
9	Orlando-Kissimmee-Sanford, FL[a]	15,267	12,638	12,501	1.90
10	San Diego-Carlsbad-San Marcos, CA[a]	14,859	11,527	11,345	1.70
11	[a,b]	14,761	12,619	12,534	1.38
12	Lakeland-Winter Haven, FL[a]	14,678	11,430	11,191	1.27
13	Seattle-Tacoma-Bellevue, WA[a]	14,644	11,654	11,491	1.37
14	Fort Wayne, IN[a]	14,543	11,690	11,690	1.44
15	Columbus, OH[a]	14,478	11,905	11,726	1.76
16	Portland-Vancouver-Hillsboro, OR-WA[a]	14,337	11,552	11,419	1.43
17	Nashville-Davidson-Murfreesboro-Franklin, TN	14,335	11,268	11,268	2.19
18	Cape Coral-Fort Myers, FL	14,327	11,706	11,585	2.32
19	[b]	14,115	11,711	11,625	1.67
20	[b]	14,042	11,450	11,341	1.90
21	Ann Arbor, MI	13,986	11,915	11,915	1.35
22	[b]	13,933	10,996	10,996	1.95
23	Akron, OH	13,788	11,251	11,251	2.64
24	Allentown-Bethlehem-Easton, PA-NJ	13,634	11,335	11,251	1.39
25	Tampa-St. Petersburg-Clearwater, FL	13,374	10,264	10,117	1.78

Rank	MSA	Average adjusted spending (in dollars)		Average for initial admission	
		Episode	Hospital inpatient services	Price (in dollars)	Days
26	Dayton, OH	12,973	10,367	10,136	1.96
27	Huntington-Ashland, WV-KY-OH	12,897	10,320	10,320	1.73
28	Detroit-Warren-Livonia, MI	12,879	10,899	10,724	1.86
29	Sacramento-Arden-Arcade-Roseville, CA	12,862	9,362	9,311	1.42
30	Chicago-Joliet-Naperville, IL-IN-WI	12,800	10,152	10,038	1.76
31	Kansas City, MO-KS	12,596	9,867	9,689	1.99
32	Cincinnati-Middletown, OH-KY-IN	12,571	10,069	9,938	1.61
33	Minneapolis-St. Paul-Bloomington, MN-WI	12,477	9,379	9,336	1.39
34	Dallas-Fort Worth-Arlington, TX	12,413	9,273	9,193	1.64
35	Raleigh-Cary, NC	12,403	9,281	9,281	1.83
36	Providence-New Bedford-Fall River, RI-MA	12,394	9,978	9,813	2.00
37	[b]	12,358	10,014	9,845	1.72
38	[b]	12,336	9,554	9,458	1.66
39	New York-Northern New Jersey-Long Island, NY-NJ-PA	12,252	7,832	7,716	1.57
40	Shreveport-Bossier City, LA	12,011	8,831	8,706	2.13
41	Birmingham-Hoover, AL	11,960	8,853	8,759	2.05
42	[b]	11,851	9,524	9,524	2.19
43	Houston-Sugar Land-Baytown, TX	11,496	8,598	8,475	1.77
44	Boston-Cambridge-Quincy, MA-NH	11,417	8,412	8,310	1.52

Table 10. (Continued)

Rank	MSA	Average adjusted spending (in dollars)		Average for initial admission	
		Episode	Hospital inpatient services	Price (in dollars)	Days
45	Phoenix-Mesa-Glendale, AZ	11,403	7,978	7,833	1.59
46	Philadelphia-Camden-Wilmington, PA-NJ-DE-MD	11,351	8,910	8,828	1.53
47	Tulsa, OK	11,314	8,976	8,626	1.50
48	Rochester, NY	11,144	8,542	8,542	2.22
49	Cleveland-Elyria-Mentor, OH	11,078	8,537	8,537	1.86
50	[b]	11,037	8,807	8,679	1.71
51	Springfield, MA	10,958	8,113	8,113	1.69
52	Lexington-Fayette, KY	10,831	8,702	8,682	1.63
53	Bridgeport-Stamford-Norwalk, CT	10,821	7,604	7,554	1.51
54	[b]	10,775	8,969	8,908	2.19
55	Louisville-Jefferson County, KY-IN	10,771	8,562	8,412	2.20
56	[b]	10,766	8,413	8,085	1.47
57	New Orleans-Metairie-Kenner, LA	10,695	7,816	7,607	1.94
58	Toledo, OH	10,693	8,249	8,040	2.00
59	[b]	10,470	7,234	7,045	1.65
60	Denver-Aurora-Broomfield, CO	10,372	7,004	6,948	1.57
61	Los Angeles-Long Beach-Santa Ana, CA	10,351	7,117	7,010	1.61
62	Memphis, TN-MS-AR	10,191	6,880	6,796	1.90
63	San Antonio-New Braunfels, TX[c]	10,163	7,580	7,430	1.83
64	[b,c]	10,116	7,122	6,880	2.03

Rank	MSA	Average adjusted spending (in dollars)		Average for initial admission	
		Episode	Hospital inpatient services	Price (in dollars)	Days
65	Riverside-San Bernardino-Ontario, CA[c]	10,108	6,935	6,728	1.72
66	Knoxville, TN[c]	9,887	6,890	6,564	2.38
67	Hartford-West Hartford-East Hartford, CT[c]	9,304	6,412	6,340	1.60
68	Savannah, GA[c]	9,281	6,727	6,575	2.18
69	Albany-Schenectady-Troy, NY[c]	8,922	6,456	6,261	1.57
70	[b,c]	8,880	6,787	6,672	1.77
71	San Jose-Sunnyvale-Santa Clara, CA[c]	8,848	5,302	5,302	1.43
72	Youngstown-Warren-Boardman, OH-PA[c]	8,747	6,857	6,857	1.72
73	Santa Rosa-Petaluma, CA[c]	8,618	5,608	5,202	1.47
74	Oxnard-Thousand Oaks-Ventura, CA[c]	7,993	5,377	5,290	1.30
75	Albuquerque, NM[c]	7,989	5,167	5,122	1.55
76	Las Vegas-Paradise, NV[c]	7,773	4,576	4,528	1.54
77	St. Louis, MO-IL[c]	7,698	5,014	4,905	1.70
78	Fresno, CA[c]	7,096	4,993	4,882	1.61

Source: GAO analysis of 2009 and 2010 claims data from Truven Health Analytics. | GAO-15-214.

Note: Data were from 78 MSAs. We included all MSAs with a sufficient number of episodes to support our analyses for all three procedures. Spending and prices were adjusted to control for geographic differences in the cost of doing business and differences in demographics and health status of enrollees in each MSA.

[a] MSA was in the highest-spending quintile. The 16 MSAs in the highest-spending quintile had an average of $13,331 in spending on hospital inpatient services.

[b] MSA name withheld to protect the confidentiality of entities that contributed private data.

[c] MSA was in the lowest-spending quintile. The 16 MSAs in the lowest-spending quintile had an average of $6,113 in spending on hospital inpatient services.

Table 11. Hospital Inpatient Spending, Initial Admission Price, and Number of Days, by Metropolitan Statistical Area (MSA), for Total Hip Replacement Episodes

Rank	MSA	Average adjusted spending (in dollars)		Average for initial admission	
		Episode	Hospital inpatient services	Price (in dollars)	Days
1	Salinas, CA[a]	57,990	52,757	52,757	3.39
2	Dallas-Fort Worth-Arlington, TX[a]	41,129	35,488	35,183	2.95
3	San Diego-Carlsbad-San Marcos, CA[a]	37,906	31,283	31,005	2.79
4	[a,b]	37,669	31,896	31,611	3.14
5	[a,b]	36,936	31,129	30,508	3.11
6	Madison, WI[a]	36,258	25,671	25,671	2.65
7	Milwaukee-Waukesha-West Allis, WI[a]	35,963	28,392	27,935	2.87
8	New York-Northern New Jersey-Long Island, NY-NJ-PA[a]	35,682	25,800	25,378	3.29
9	Houston-Sugar Land-Baytown, TX[a]	35,332	29,510	29,231	2.93
10	San Antonio-New Braunfels, TX[a]	35,319	30,041	29,734	2.93
11	Fort Wayne, IN[a]	34,711	30,406	30,140	2.45
12	Sacramento-Arden-Arcade-Roseville, CA[a]	34,420	27,594	27,594	2.93
13	Nashville-Davidson-Murfreesboro-Franklin, TN[a]	34,311	28,079	27,886	2.59
14	[a,b]	33,899	28,450	28,450	3.38
15	Albany-Schenectady-Troy, NY[a]	32,246	26,505	26,246	2.38
16	[a,b]	31,726	26,125	25,983	2.74
17	Colorado Springs, CO	31,648	26,345	26,135	2.49
18	[b]	31,550	25,757	25,360	2.78
19	Charleston, WV	31,376	25,999	25,604	2.46

Rank	MSA	Average adjusted spending (in dollars)		Average for initial admission	
		Episode	Hospital inpatient services	Price (in dollars)	Days
20	[b]	31,371	25,170	24,840	3.25
21	Portland-Vancouver-Hillsboro, OR-WA	30,535	25,071	24,880	2.48
22	Orlando-Kissimmee-Sanford, FL	30,473	25,314	25,127	3.22
23	Cape Coral-Fort Myers, FL	30,422	25,235	25,103	2.75
24	Seattle-Tacoma-Bellevue, WA	30,398	24,612	24,406	2.75
25	Tampa-St. Petersburg-Clearwater, FL	30,380	24,265	23,762	3.16
26	[b]	30,205	22,953	22,389	3.02
27	[b]	30,072	24,631	24,210	3.20
28	[b]	29,817	24,239	24,154	2.86
29	Lakeland-Winter Haven, FL	29,480	23,488	23,127	2.82
30	Knoxville, TN	29,470	24,060	23,862	2.45
31	Memphis, TN-MS-AR	29,073	22,607	22,198	3.18
32	New Orleans-Metairie-Kenner, LA	29,035	23,439	22,986	3.05
33	San Jose-Sunnyvale-Santa Clara, CA	28,626	22,145	21,967	3.00
34	Raleigh-Cary, NC	28,162	22,407	22,407	3.03
35	[b]	28,090	22,561	22,368	2.62
36	Huntington-Ashland, WV-KY-OH	28,065	22,695	22,522	2.88
37	Denver-Aurora-Broomfield, CO	28,042	22,545	22,355	2.66
38	Providence-New Bedford-Fall River, RI-MA	27,936	21,568	21,392	3.64
39	Chicago-Joliet-Naperville, IL-IN-WI	27,774	21,231	21,060	2.95
40	Kansas City, MO-KS	27,770	22,098	21,944	2.84
41	Ann Arbor, MI	27,709	22,896	22,539	3.44

Table 11. (Continued)

Rank	MSA	Average adjusted spending (in dollars)		Average for initial admission	
		Episode	Hospital inpatient services	Price (in dollars)	Days
42	Philadelphia-Camden-Wilmington, PA-NJ-DE-MD	27,354	21,643	21,300	2.67
43	Detroit-Warren-Livonia, MI	26,945	21,762	21,404	3.10
44	Savannah, GA	26,937	20,052	19,912	2.12
45	Cincinnati-Middletown, OH-KY-IN	26,868	21,591	21,338	2.76
46	Bridgeport-Stamford-Norwalk, CT	26,858	19,894	19,823	3.33
47	Phoenix-Mesa-Glendale, AZ	26,856	20,222	19,995	2.55
48	Tulsa, OK	26,651	21,459	21,318	2.12
49	Minneapolis-St. Paul-Bloomington, MN-WI	26,628	19,928	19,649	2.78
50	Boston-Cambridge-Quincy, MA-NH	26,618	20,720	20,568	3.47
51	Shreveport-Bossier City, LA	26,580	20,471	20,181	2.94
52	[b]	26,557	20,284	20,093	3.21
53	Albuquerque, NM	26,481	20,098	20,001	3.22
54	Cleveland-Elyria-Mentor, OH	25,683	20,483	20,256	3.06
55	Columbus, OH	25,627	21,205	20,977	2.28
56	[b]	25,409	19,379	19,193	2.92
57	Los Angeles-Long Beach-Santa Ana, CA	24,972	19,558	19,380	2.66
58	Springfield, MA	24,914	19,062	18,964	3.37
59	Oxnard-Thousand Oaks-Ventura, CA	24,908	18,695	18,565	2.78
60	Santa Rosa-Petaluma, CA	24,548	17,284	17,284	2.78
61	Las Vegas-Paradise, NV	24,490	18,655	17,986	3.10

Rank	MSA	Average adjusted spending (in dollars)		Average for initial admission	
		Episode	Hospital inpatient services	Price (in dollars)	Days
62	Grand Rapids-Wyoming, MI	24,475	19,899	19,580	2.76
63	Rochester, NY[c]	24,365	19,508	19,266	2.91
64	Louisville-Jefferson County, KY-IN[c]	24,199	19,258	19,155	2.84
65	Allentown-Bethlehem-Easton, PA-NJ[c]	24,117	18,181	17,938	3.00
66	[b,c]	23,894	17,750	17,457	2.85
67	St. Louis, MO-IL[c]	23,816	18,817	18,557	2.65
68	Dayton, OH[c]	23,614	18,820	18,670	2.80
69	Riverside-San Bernardino-Ontario, CA[c]	23,361	18,457	18,183	3.13
70	[b,c]	23,314	18,492	18,262	2.88
71	Akron, OH[c]	23,100	19,155	18,886	3.14
72	Hartford-West Hartford-East Hartford, CT[c]	22,478	16,600	16,388	2.86
73	Lexington-Fayette, KY[c]	22,274	17,646	17,646	2.75
74	Toledo, OH[c]	22,242	17,487	17,160	2.78
75	Fresno, CA[c]	20,508	16,380	16,352	2.04
76	[b,c]	19,794	14,410	14,243	3.09
77	Birmingham-Hoover, AL[c]	19,166	12,103	12,036	2.81
78	Youngstown-Warren-Boardman, OH-PA[c]	19,164	14,095	13,945	3.42

Source: GAO analysis of 2009 and 2010 claims data from Truven Health Analytics. | GAO-15-214.

Note: Data were from 78 MSAs. We included all MSAs with a sufficient number of episodes to support our analyses for all three procedures. Spending and prices were adjusted to control for geographic differences in the cost of doing business and differences in demographics and health status of enrollees in each MSA.

[a] MSA was in the highest-spending quintile. The 16 MSAs in the highest-spending quintile had an average of $30,570 in spending on hospital inpatient services.

[b] MSA name withheld to protect the confidentiality of entities that contributed private data.

[c] MSA was in the lowest-spending quintile. The 16 MSAs in the lowest-spending quintile had an average of $17,323 in spending on hospital inpatient services.

APPENDIX VI. PROFESSIONAL SERVICES SPENDING AND OTHER INFORMATION, BY METROPOLITAN STATISTICAL AREA AND PROCEDURE

This appendix presents professional service spending, number of services, intensity, and price, by metropolitan statistical area (MSA), for each of the three high-cost procedures we analyzed—coronary stent placement, laparoscopic appendectomy, and total hip replacement.

Table 12. Professional Services Spending, Number of Services, Intensity, and Price, by Metropolitan Statistical Area (MSA), for Coronary Stent Placement Episodes

Rank	MSA	Average adjusted spending (in dollars)		Average for professional services		
		Episode	Professional services	Volume (number of services)	Intensity	Price per unit of intensity (in dollars)
1	Salinas, CA[a]	60,375	4,454	16.25	3.93	69.76
2	[a,b]	39,827	3,278	14.22	4.02	57.34
3	Charleston, WV[a]	39,782	3,403	15.28	5.04	44.16
4	San Diego-Carlsbad-San Marcos, CA[a]	39,683	4,481	15.34	3.97	73.48
5	Milwaukee-Waukesha-West Allis, WI[a]	38,596	5,833	14.65	3.93	101.21
6	Albany-Schenectady-Troy, NY[a]	38,305	2,614	15.64	3.84	43.54
7	Madison, WI[a]	37,248	9,022	11.60	4.18	186.03
8	[a,b]	36,858	3,422	13.14	4.12	63.14
9	Houston-Sugar Land-Baytown, TX[a]	36,097	3,523	16.80	3.87	54.13
10	[a,b]	35,478	3,054	14.87	4.93	41.66
11	Providence-New Bedford-Fall River, RI-MA[a]	35,358	3,135	17.87	3.53	49.67

Rank	MSA	Average adjusted spending (in dollars)		Average for professional services		
		Episode	Professional services	Volume (number of services)	Intensity	Price per unit of intensity (in dollars)
12	Seattle-Tacoma-Bellevue, WA[a]	34,388	3,499	10.37	3.71	91.05
13	Fort Wayne, IN[a]	34,307	3,373	14.94	3.76	60.05
14	Nashville-Davidson-Murfreesboro-Franklin, TN[a]	34,258	3,356	13.77	3.96	61.48
15	[a,b]	33,974	2,683	11.22	4.43	53.92
16	Allentown-Bethlehem-Easton, PA-NJ[a]	33,398	3,117	15.64	4.78	41.72
17	Sacramento-Arden-Arcade-Roseville, CA	32,807	4,006	15.29	3.79	69.08
18	Orlando-Kissimmee-Sanford, FL	32,605	2,842	15.88	3.90	45.93
19	Tampa-St. Petersburg-Clearwater, FL	32,156	2,765	16.20	3.94	43.29
20	Cape Coral-Fort Myers, FL	32,143	3,020	17.65	3.73	45.84
21	Kansas City, MO-KS	32,068	3,189	14.34	3.98	55.90
22	Raleigh-Cary, NC	31,879	3,603	14.89	4.07	59.49
23	Dallas-Fort Worth-Arlington, TX	31,847	3,021	15.20	3.88	51.26
24	San Jose-Sunnyvale-Santa Clara, CA	31,797	4,464	16.11	3.92	70.74
25	Colorado Springs, CO	31,017	2,902	13.88	4.08	51.28
26	[b]	30,680	3,371	16.00	4.83	43.58
27	Memphis, TN-MS-AR	30,607	4,178	15.61	3.62	73.91
28	[b]	30,243	3,161	14.67	3.74	57.67
29	[b]	30,156	4,544	14.91	4.02	75.84
30	Fresno, CA	29,925	2,546	15.63	3.96	41.08

Table 12. (Continued)

Rank	MSA	Average adjusted spending (in dollars)		Average for professional services		
		Episode	Professional services	Volume (number of services)	Intensity	Price per unit of intensity (in dollars)
31	Grand Rapids-Wyoming, MI	29,684	2,764	14.31	3.80	50.83
32	Philadelphia-Camden-Wilmington, PA-NJ-DE-MD	29,489	2,899	14.05	4.22	48.92
33	[b]	29,393	3,255	13.94	3.89	60.06
34	Ann Arbor, MI	29,302	3,084	16.60	3.67	50.59
35	Denver-Aurora-Broomfield, CO	28,698	3,157	16.04	3.86	50.95
36	Chicago-Joliet-Naperville, IL-IN-WI	28,640	3,414	16.08	3.94	53.85
37	New York-Northern New Jersey-Long Island, NY-NJ-PA	28,629	3,196	15.31	3.93	53.15
38	Lakeland-Winter Haven, FL	28,607	3,538	16.67	3.74	56.69
39	Portland-Vancouver-Hillsboro, OR-WA	28,553	4,179	13.51	4.15	74.50
40	Boston-Cambridge-Quincy, MA-NH	28,474	3,648	16.13	3.75	60.36
41	[b]	28,276	2,891	15.47	3.82	48.88
42	Santa Rosa-Petaluma, CA	28,065	4,651	16.24	3.82	75.05
43	Huntington-Ashland, WV-KY-OH	27,705	2,725	15.73	4.08	42.42
44	Detroit-Warren-Livonia, MI	27,544	2,747	17.27	3.67	43.28
45	San Antonio-New Braunfels, TX	27,489	2,688	15.93	4.10	41.16

Rank	MSA	Average adjusted spending (in dollars)		Average for professional services		
		Episode	Professional services	Volume (number of services)	Intensity	Price per unit of intensity (in dollars)
46	New Orleans-Metairie-Kenner, LA	27,480	3,324	16.48	3.57	56.44
47	Minneapolis-St. Paul-Bloomington, MN-WI	27,308	4,788	14.22	4.20	80.21
48	Phoenix-Mesa-Glendale, AZ	27,067	3,581	15.22	4.33	54.31
49	[b]	26,746	2,991	14.25	4.05	51.83
50	[b]	26,349	3,327	15.23	3.51	62.27
51	Rochester, NY	25,523	2,587	12.88	4.11	48.82
52	Riverside-San Bernardino-Ontario, CA	25,322	3,638	15.48	4.16	56.53
53	St. Louis, MO-IL	25,288	2,982	14.95	3.94	50.66
54	Toledo, OH	25,210	2,934	14.42	3.95	51.58
55	Cincinnati-Middletown, OH-KY-IN	25,203	2,866	15.18	3.90	48.42
56	Albuquerque, NM	25,015	3,264	15.54	3.84	54.64
57	Cleveland-Elyria-Mentor, OH	24,914	3,004	15.83	3.81	49.79
58	Shreveport-Bossier City, LA	24,848	4,818	14.10	4.16	82.16
59	[b]	24,753	3,610	12.93	4.29	65.07
60	Columbus, OH	24,310	2,476	14.71	3.79	44.37
61	Tulsa, OK	24,088	2,990	14.24	4.07	51.54
62	[b]	23,938	3,753	11.93	4.44	70.79
63	Knoxville, TN[c]	23,935	4,027	16.27	3.62	68.31
64	[b,c]	23,647	2,907	17.21	4.70	35.90
65	Bridgeport-Stamford-Norwalk, CT[c]	23,135	3,248	14.58	3.99	55.80

Table 12. (Continued)

Rank	MSA	Average adjusted spending (in dollars)		Average for professional services		
		Episode	Professional services	Volume (number of services)	Intensity	Price per unit of intensity (in dollars)
66	Los Angeles-Long Beach-Santa Ana, CA[c]	22,768	3,207	15.49	3.91	53.00
67	Savannah, GA[c]	22,585	3,274	13.78	4.13	57.51
68	Hartford-West Hartford -East Hartford, CT[c]	22,357	3,276	16.07	3.65	55.83
69	Dayton, OH[c]	22,073	2,661	15.17	4.02	43.64
70	Oxnard-Thousand Oaks-Ventura, CA[c]	22,023	3,465	15.30	4.26	53.18
71	Springfield, MA[c]	21,937	3,593	20.95	3.14	54.70
72	[b,c]	21,664	2,712	16.72	4.90	33.10
73	Akron, OH[c]	21,664	2,506	15.31	3.74	43.72
74	Las Vegas-Paradise, NV[c]	20,969	3,019	20.50	3.61	40.78
75	Lexington-Fayette, KY[c]	20,602	2,140	13.11	3.97	41.06
76	Youngstown-Warren-Boardman, OH-PA[c]	18,829	2,677	18.54	3.97	36.34
77	Louisville-Jefferson County, KY-IN[c]	18,677	2,534	17.94	3.62	38.97
78	Birmingham-Hoover, AL[c]	17,768	4,339	14.59	4.27	69.64

Source: GAO analysis of 2009 and 2010 claims data from Truven Health Analytics. | GAO-15-214.

Note: Data were from 78 MSAs. We included all MSAs with a sufficient number of episodes to support our analyses for all three procedures. Spending, volume, and intensity were adjusted to control for differences in demographics and health status of enrollees in each MSA; spending was also adjusted for geographic differences in the cost of doing business. Intensity was measured by the relative value unit (RVU) assigned to each service.

[a] MSA was in the highest-spending quintile. The 16 MSAs in the highest-spending quintile had an average of $3,890 in spending on professional services. For those professional services, the 16 MSAs had an average of 14.48 services, average intensity of 4.13, and average price per unit of intensity of $68.27.

[b] MSA name withheld to protect the confidentiality of entities that contributed private data.

[c] MSA was in the lowest-spending quintile. The 16 MSAs in the lowest-spending quintile had an average of $3,099 in spending on professional services. For those professional services, the 16 MSAs had an average of 16.35 services, average intensity of 3.97, and average price per unit of intensity of $48.84.

Table 13. Professional Services Spending, Number of Services, Intensity, and Price, by Metropolitan Statistical Area (MSA), for Laparoscopic Appendectomy Episodes

Rank	MSA	Average adjusted spending (in dollars)		Average for professional services		
		Episode	Professional services	Volume (number of services)	Intensity	Price per unit of intensity (in dollars)
1	Salinas, CA[a]	25,924	2,106	5.06	5.51	75.59
2	Madison, WI[a]	18,123	4,090	4.45	5.67	161.98
3	Milwaukee-Waukesha-West Allis, WI[a]	18,096	3,752	4.68	5.77	138.82
4	Charleston, WV[a]	17,640	2,632	4.16	6.45	98.06
5	[a,b]	16,588	2,613	4.75	5.77	95.28
6	[a,b]	16,323	2,104	3.53	6.51	91.45
7	Grand Rapids-Wyoming, MI[a]	15,444	2,058	4.54	6.42	70.67
8	Colorado Springs, CO[a]	15,318	4,054	4.38	5.95	155.40
9	Orlando-Kissimmee-Sanford, FL[a]	15,267	2,423	5.20	5.77	80.79
10	San Diego-Carlsbad-San Marcos, CA[a]	14,859	3,130	5.19	5.64	106.89

Table 13. (Continued)

Rank	MSA	Average adjusted spending (in dollars)		Average for professional services		
		Episode	Professional services	Volume (number of services)	Intensity	Price per unit of intensity (in dollars)
11	[a,b]	14,761	1,999	4.03	6.31	78.63
12	Lakeland-Winter Haven, FL[a]	14,678	2,873	5.22	6.11	89.99
13	Seattle-Tacoma-Bellevue, WA[a]	14,644	2,814	4.13	5.17	131.72
14	Fort Wayne, IN[a]	14,543	2,178	4.37	6.02	82.70
15	Columbus, OH[a]	14,478	2,153	4.80	5.62	79.83
16	Portland-Vancouver-Hillsboro, OR-WA[a]	14,337	2,644	4.63	5.68	100.45
17	Nashville-Davidson-Murfreesboro-Franklin, TN	14,335	2,831	4.87	5.75	100.97
18	Cape Coral-Fort Myers, FL	14,327	2,445	5.55	5.88	74.89
19	[b]	14,115	2,196	3.45	6.44	99.00
20	[b]	14,042	2,273	5.08	5.40	82.86
21	Ann Arbor, MI	13,986	1,969	5.05	5.67	68.82
22	[b]	13,933	2,508	4.40	6.16	92.51
23	Akron, OH	13,788	2,177	5.66	5.21	73.83
24	Allentown-Bethlehem-Easton, PA-NJ	13,634	2,095	6.16	4.76	71.40
25	Tampa-St. Petersburg-Clearwater, FL	13,374	2,761	6.23	5.19	85.26
26	Dayton, OH	12,973	2,449	5.40	5.55	81.69
27	Huntington-Ashland, WV-KY-OH	12,897	2,229	4.72	5.95	79.30
28	Detroit-Warren-Livonia, MI	12,879	1,801	5.07	5.40	65.82

Rank	MSA	Average adjusted spending (in dollars)		Average for professional services		
		Episode	Professional services	Volume (number of services)	Intensity	Price per unit of intensity (in dollars)
29	Sacramento-Arden-Arcade-Roseville, CA	12,862	3,257	5.09	5.56	115.17
30	Chicago-Joliet-Naperville, IL-IN-WI	12,800	2,377	5.44	5.53	79.13
31	Kansas City, MO-KS	12,596	2,436	5.92	5.34	77.04
32	Cincinnati-Middletown, OH-KY-IN	12,571	2,365	4.85	5.77	84.40
33	Minneapolis-St. Paul-Bloomington, MN-WI	12,477	2,951	5.50	5.20	103.29
34	Dallas-Fort Worth-Arlington, TX	12,413	2,854	4.69	5.86	103.99
35	Raleigh-Cary, NC	12,403	2,803	4.56	6.07	101.15
36	Providence-New Bedford-Fall River, RI-MA	12,394	2,309	5.01	5.43	84.84
37	[b]	12,358	2,107	3.41	6.92	89.23
38	[b]	12,336	2,379	4.20	6.29	90.21
39	New York-Northern New Jersey-Long Island, NY-NJ-PA	12,252	4,250	5.77	5.22	141.25
40	Shreveport-Bossier City, LA	12,011	3,008	5.09	5.49	107.60
41	Birmingham-Hoover, AL	11,960	2,835	4.29	6.05	109.22
42	[b]	11,851	2,172	6.21	4.97	70.38
43	Houston-Sugar Land-Baytown, TX	11,496	2,492	4.93	5.68	88.96
44	Boston-Cambridge-Quincy, MA-NH	11,417	2,777	4.67	5.76	103.22
45	Phoenix-Mesa-Glendale, AZ	11,403	3,194	6.37	5.14	97.47

Table 13. (Continued)

Rank	MSA	Average adjusted spending (in dollars)		Average for professional services		
		Episode	Professional services	Volume (number of services)	Intensity	Price per unit of intensity (in dollars)
46	Philadelphia-Camden-Wilmington, PA-NJ-DE-MD	11,351	2,266	5.08	5.54	80.53
47	Tulsa, OK	11,314	2,050	3.51	7.21	81.08
48	Rochester, NY	11,144	2,456	4.13	6.32	94.11
49	Cleveland-Elyria-Mentor, OH	11,078	2,300	4.54	5.95	85.17
50	[b]	11,037	1,975	5.44	5.31	68.36
51	Springfield, MA	10,958	2,660	4.73	5.82	96.57
52	Lexington-Fayette, KY	10,831	1,910	4.64	5.86	70.23
53	Bridgeport-Stamford-Norwalk, CT	10,821	2,941	5.16	5.30	107.53
54	[b]	10,775	1,613	3.72	5.99	72.42
55	Louisville-Jefferson County, KY-IN	10,771	1,929	4.88	5.90	67.05
56	[b]	10,766	2,139	6.44	8.49	39.14
57	New Orleans-Metairie-Kenner, LA	10,695	2,563	5.16	5.44	91.40
58	Toledo, OH	10,693	2,285	6.37	4.87	73.61
59	[b]	10,470	3,041	5.08	5.53	108.20
60	Denver-Aurora-Broomfield, CO	10,372	3,043	4.96	5.46	112.29
61	Los Angeles-Long Beach-Santa Ana, CA	10,351	3,020	6.21	5.03	96.65
62	Memphis, TN-MS-AR	10,191	3,122	4.86	5.95	107.95
63	San Antonio-New Braunfels, TX[c]	10,163	2,364	5.27	5.41	82.85
64	[b,c]	10,116	2,828	3.91	6.10	118.54

Rank	MSA	Average adjusted spending (in dollars)		Average for professional services		
		Episode	Professional services	Volume (number of services)	Intensity	Price per unit of intensity (in dollars)
65	Riverside-San Bernardino-Ontario, CA[c]	10,108	2,907	5.48	5.26	100.73
66	Knoxville, TN[c]	9,887	2,820	5.30	5.21	102.16
67	Hartford-West Hartford - East Hartford, CT[c]	9,304	2,726	4.59	5.83	101.79
68	Savannah, GA[c]	9,281	2,388	4.33	6.13	90.02
69	Albany-Schenectady-Troy, NY[c]	8,922	2,338	4.90	5.96	80.11
70	[b,c]	8,880	1,924	6.14	5.14	60.98
71	San Jose-Sunnyvale-Santa Clara, CA[c]	8,848	3,273	5.54	5.19	113.79
72	Youngstown-Warren-Boardman, OH-PA[c]	8,747	1,765	5.33	5.34	62.06
73	Santa Rosa-Petaluma, CA[c]	8,618	2,780	5.38	5.43	95.23
74	Oxnard-Thousand Oaks-Ventura, CA[c]	7,993	2,449	6.21	4.96	79.43
75	Albuquerque, NM[c]	7,989	2,631	4.73	5.68	98.04
76	Las Vegas-Paradise, NV[c]	7,773	2,982	6.54	5.09	89.66
77	St. Louis, MO-IL[c]	7,698	2,448	4.97	5.58	88.14
78	Fresno, CA[c]	7,096	1,935	5.01	5.65	68.30

Source: GAO analysis of 2009 and 2010 claims data from Truven Health Analytics. | GAO-15-214.

Note: Data were from 78 MSAs. We included all MSAs with a sufficient number of episodes to support our analyses for all three procedures. Spending, volume, and intensity were adjusted to control for differences in demographics and health status of enrollees in each MSA; spending was also adjusted for geographic differences in the cost of doing business. Intensity was measured by the relative value unit (RVU) assigned to each service.

[a] MSA was in the highest-spending quintile. The 16 MSAs in the highest-spending quintile had an average of $2,726 in spending on professional services. For those

professional services, the 16 MSAs had an average of 4.57 services, average intensity of 5.90, and average price per unit of intensity of $102.39.

[b] MSA name withheld to protect the confidentiality of entities that contributed private data.

[c] MSA was in the lowest-spending quintile. The 16 MSAs in the lowest-spending quintile had an average of $2,535 in spending on professional services. For those professional services, the 16 MSAs had an average of 5.23 services, average intensity of 5.50, and average price per unit of intensity of $89.49.

Table 14. Professional Services Spending, Number of Services, Intensity, and Price, by Metropolitan Statistical Area (MSA), for Total Hip Replacement Episodes

Rank	MSA	Average adjusted spending (in dollars)		Average for professional services		
		Episode	Professional services	Volume (number of services)	Intensity	Price per unit of intensity (in dollars)
1	Salinas, CA[a]	57,990	4,048	8.30	6.52	74.72
2	Dallas-Fort Worth-Arlington, TX[a]	41,129	4,181	8.35	6.68	74.91
3	San Diego-Carlsbad-San Marcos, CA[a]	37,906	5,450	8.74	6.38	97.81
4	[a,b]	37,669	4,792	13.05	4.89	75.05
5	[a,b]	36,936	4,450	6.78	7.49	87.72
6	Madison, WI[a]	36,258	9,794	5.11	9.47	202.36
7	Milwaukee-Waukesha-West Allis, WI[a]	35,963	6,774	6.67	7.78	130.68
8	New York-Northern New Jersey-Long Island, NY-NJ-PA[a]	35,682	7,839	14.23	4.46	123.44
9	Houston-Sugar Land-Baytown, TX[a]	35,332	5,003	10.08	5.92	83.92
10	San Antonio-New Braunfels, TX[a]	35,319	4,099	15.03	4.03	67.62

Rank	MSA	Average adjusted spending (in dollars)		Average for professional services		
		Episode	Professional services	Volume (number of services)	Intensity	Price per unit of intensity (in dollars)
11	Fort Wayne, IN[a]	34,711	3,978	4.84	10.07	81.70
12	Sacramento-Arden-Arcade-Roseville, CA[a]	34,420	4,741	7.12	7.76	85.80
13	Nashville-Davidson-Murfreesboro-Franklin, TN[a]	34,311	5,103	13.31	4.27	89.68
14	[a,b]	33,899	4,306	7.91	6.33	86.03
15	Albany-Schenectady-Troy, NY[a]	32,246	4,335	9.42	5.82	79.01
16	[a,b]	31,726	4,642	6.64	7.47	93.58
17	Colorado Springs, CO	31,648	4,383	11.30	4.91	79.01
18	[b]	31,550	4,792	6.42	7.98	93.59
19	Charleston, WV	31,376	5,079	8.33	5.83	104.53
20	[b]	31,371	5,052	11.08	5.22	87.39
21	Portland-Vancouver-Hillsboro, OR-WA	30,535	4,882	6.66	8.12	90.19
22	Orlando-Kissimmee-Sanford, FL	30,473	3,857	9.66	6.32	63.16
23	Cape Coral-Fort Myers, FL	30,422	3,797	7.40	7.18	71.40
24	Seattle-Tacoma-Bellevue, WA	30,398	4,961	5.53	6.68	134.30
25	Tampa-St. Petersburg-Clearwater, FL	30,380	4,225	9.92	5.99	71.16
26	[b]	30,205	5,688	7.78	6.99	104.61
27	[b]	30,072	4,345	11.73	15.45	23.97
28	[b]	29,817	4,335	9.61	5.76	78.39
29	Lakeland-Winter Haven, FL	29,480	4,029	7.85	10.46	49.05
30	Knoxville, TN	29,470	4,664	8.44	6.22	88.93

Table 14. (Continued)

Rank	MSA	Average adjusted spending (in dollars)		Average for professional services		
		Episode	Professional services	Volume (number of services)	Intensity	Price per unit of intensity (in dollars)
31	Memphis, TN-MS-AR	29,073	5,566	12.28	4.51	100.39
32	New Orleans-Metairie-Kenner, LA	29,035	4,022	8.16	6.87	71.68
33	San Jose-Sunnyvale-Santa Clara, CA	28,626	5,681	8.47	6.55	102.36
34	Raleigh-Cary, NC	28,162	4,623	7.64	7.73	78.27
35	[b]	28,090	4,487	9.52	5.94	79.35
36	Huntington-Ashland, WV-KY-OH	28,065	4,212	7.51	8.44	66.41
37	Denver-Aurora-Broomfield, CO	28,042	4,663	10.83	6.02	71.46
38	Providence-New Bedford-Fall River, RI-MA	27,936	4,667	8.28	6.58	85.70
39	Chicago-Joliet-Naperville, IL-IN-WI	27,774	5,042	12.56	4.91	81.76
40	Kansas City, MO-KS	27,770	4,197	9.48	6.71	65.92
41	Ann Arbor, MI	27,709	3,784	7.13	7.40	71.76
42	Philadelphia-Camden-Wilmington, PA-NJ-DE-MD	27,354	4,452	12.18	4.72	77.41
43	Detroit-Warren-Livonia, MI	26,945	3,704	9.97	5.57	66.73
44	Savannah, GA	26,937	4,590	6.17	8.57	86.71
45	Cincinnati-Middletown, OH-KY-IN	26,868	4,231	10.85	5.09	76.59
46	Bridgeport-Stamford-Norwalk, CT	26,858	6,051	12.67	4.58	104.35

Rank	MSA	Average adjusted spending (in dollars)		Average for professional services		
		Episode	Professional services	Volume (number of services)	Intensity	Price per unit of intensity (in dollars)
47	Phoenix-Mesa-Glendale, AZ	26,856	5,394	11.21	6.10	78.87
48	Tulsa, OK	26,651	4,136	7.14	8.15	71.06
49	Minneapolis-St. Paul-Bloomington, MN-WI	26,628	6,107	7.82	6.78	115.13
50	Boston-Cambridge-Quincy, MA-NH	26,618	4,353	7.39	6.96	84.64
51	Shreveport-Bossier City, LA	26,580	5,292	8.00	6.74	98.06
52	[b]	26,557	5,229	10.76	5.33	91.20
53	Albuquerque, NM	26,481	5,099	6.91	7.88	93.65
54	Cleveland-Elyria-Mentor, OH	25,683	4,037	9.23	6.09	71.73
55	Columbus, OH	25,627	3,717	9.15	6.05	67.19
56	[b]	25,409	5,168	4.46	11.04	104.92
57	Los Angeles-Long Beach-Santa Ana, CA	24,972	4,432	10.00	5.86	75.59
58	Springfield, MA	24,914	4,570	7.71	7.14	83.01
59	Oxnard-Thousand Oaks-Ventura, CA	24,908	4,160	11.05	5.03	74.76
60	Santa Rosa-Petaluma, CA	24,548	5,962	11.09	4.99	107.64
61	Las Vegas-Paradise, NV	24,490	4,815	16.18	4.51	65.98
62	Grand Rapids-Wyoming, MI	24,475	4,178	6.55	7.76	82.26
63	Rochester, NY[c]	24,365	3,340	5.95	9.18	61.17
64	Louisville-Jefferson County, KY-IN[c]	24,199	3,816	8.89	6.52	65.87
65	Allentown-Bethlehem-Easton, PA-NJ[c]	24,117	4,530	14.13	4.47	71.81

Table 14. (Continued)

Rank	MSA	Average adjusted spending (in dollars)		Average for professional services		
		Episode	Professional services	Volume (number of services)	Intensity	Price per unit of intensity (in dollars)
66	[b,c]	23,894	5,745	8.00	6.98	102.79
67	St. Louis, MO-IL[c]	23,816	3,804	7.37	7.14	72.26
68	Dayton, OH[c]	23,614	3,925	7.33	8.49	63.08
69	Riverside-San Bernardino-Ontario, CA[c]	23,361	3,855	9.15	5.97	70.55
70	[b,c]	23,314	3,880	12.93	4.19	71.67
71	Akron, OH[c]	23,100	3,110	9.33	5.58	59.78
72	Hartford-West Hartford-East Hartford, CT[c]	22,478	4,924	8.33	7.10	83.32
73	Lexington-Fayette, KY[c]	22,274	3,817	10.77	5.44	65.19
74	Toledo, OH[c]	22,242	4,286	14.92	4.08	70.34
75	Fresno, CA[c]	20,508	3,732	13.05	4.64	61.66
76	[b,c]	19,794	4,018	15.52	3.90	66.41
77	Birmingham-Hoover, AL[c]	19,166	5,827	9.56	6.06	100.68
78	Youngstown-Warren-Boardman, OH-PA[c]	19,164	3,893	15.72	3.91	63.28

Source: GAO analysis of 2009 and 2010 claims data from Truven Health Analytics. | GAO-15-214.

Note: Data were from 78 MSAs. We included all MSAs with a sufficient number of episodes to support our analyses for all three procedures. Spending, volume, and intensity were adjusted to control for differences in demographics and health status of enrollees in each MSA; spending was also adjusted for geographic differences in the cost of doing business. Intensity was measured by the relative value unit (RVU) assigned to each service.

[a] MSA was in the highest-spending quintile. The 16 MSAs in the highest-spending quintile had an average of $5,221 in spending on professional services. For those professional services, the 16 MSAs had an average of 9.10 services, average intensity of 6.58, and average price per unit of intensity of $95.88.

[b] MSA name withheld to protect the confidentiality of entities that contributed private data.

[c] MSA was in the lowest-spending quintile. The 16 MSAs in the lowest-spending quintile had an average of $4,157 in spending on professional services. For those professional services, the 16 MSAs had an average of 10.68 services, average intensity of 5.85, and average price per unit of intensity of $71.86.

End Notes

[1] See Centers for Medicare & Medicaid Services, *Table 1: National Health Expenditures and Selected Economic Indicators, Levels and Annual Percent Change: Calendar Years 2007-2023*, accessed October 28, 2014, http://www.cms.gov/Research-Statistics-Data- and-Systems/Statistics-Trends-and- Reports/NationalHealthExpendData/Downloads/Proj2013 tables.zip.

[2] See, for example, E. Fisher et al., "The Implications of Regional Variations in Medicare Spending. Part 1: The Content, Quality, and Accessibility of Care," *Annals of Internal Medicine*, vol. 138, no.4 (2003).

[3] Medicare is the federally financed health insurance program for persons aged 65 and over, certain individuals with disabilities, and individuals with end-stage renal disease.

[4] In 2012, private sector spending accounted for $917 billion of the $2.8 trillion in overall national health expenditures.

[5] Volume is the number of services used, and intensity is the resources needed to provide a service—for example, a 30-minute office visit has greater intensity than a 15-minute office visit.

[6] The Office of Management and Budget defines MSAs as having at least one urbanized area with a population of 50,000 or more, plus adjacent territory that has a high degree of social and economic integration with the core. Office of Management and Budget, Executive Office of the President, OMB Bulletin No. 13-01, *Revised Delineations of Metropolitan Statistical Areas, Micropolitan Statistical Areas, and Combined Statistical Areas, and Guidance on Uses of the Delineations of These Areas* (Washington, D.C.: Feb. 28, 2013).

[7] Coronary stent placement, also known as percutaneous transluminal coronary angioplasty, is a surgical cardiology procedure to open a blocked coronary artery and insert a stent (an expandable metal coil) into the newly opened artery to help prevent renarrowing or reclosure. Laparoscopic appendectomy is a general surgical procedure to remove an infected appendix using instruments placed into small abdominal incisions. Total hip replacement, also known as total hip arthroplasty, is a surgical orthopedic procedure where cartilage and bone from the hip joint are replaced with prosthetic components.

[8] These procedures also have high levels of volume among all patients in the United States. For example, according to the Healthcare Cost and Utilization Project, which includes data for all privately insured, Medicare, Medicaid, uninsured, and all other patients, these 3 procedures were among the 20 procedures with the most discharges in 2009. During that year, there were approximately 614,000 discharges for coronary stent placement, approximately 200,000 discharges for laparoscopic appendectomy, and approximately 274,000 discharges for total hip replacement.

[9] In 2012, about one-third of all health care spending in the United States was for hospital services. Spending for professional services represented over one-quarter of spending, and the remainder of spending included services such as prescription drugs, nursing home care, and home health care, as well as administrative costs. See Centers for Medicare & Medicaid Services, *Table 2: National Health Expenditures; Aggregate and Per Capita Amounts,*

Annual Percent Change and Percent Distribution, by Type of Expenditure: Selected Calendar Years 1960-2012, accessed October 28, 2014, http://www.cms.gov/Research-Statistics-Data-and-Systems/Statistics-Trends-and- Reports/NationalHealthExpendData/Downloads/tables.pdf.

[10] Specifically, we included any outpatient services received by an enrollee in the 3 days prior to admission at the same hospital where the inpatient admission occurred, because those services may be related to the admission.

[11] We excluded MSAs that had fewer than 24 coronary stent placement episodes, fewer than 17 laparoscopic appendectomy episodes, or fewer than 24 total hip replacement episodes. We had a sufficient number of episodes to support our analyses of coronary stent placement in 155 MSAs, laparoscopic appendectomy in 139 MSAs, and total hip replacement in 141 MSAs. For some analyses where we drew comparisons across procedures, we reported data on only those MSAs that had a sufficient number of episodes for all three procedures, and 78 MSAs fell into this category. We took steps to remove and limit the effect of atypical episodes. For example, we excluded enrollees who received the procedure more than one time during the episode, enrollees whose overall initial hospital admission was coded as being for a reason unrelated to the procedure analyzed, enrollees with diagnoses of end-stage renal disease, enrollees who were pregnant, and enrollees with a hospice stay.

[12] "Enrollee" also refers to any dependents, unless otherwise specified. To control for geographic differences in the cost of doing business, we applied Medicare's payment- adjustment methodology—the Geographic Practice Cost Index or the Hospital Wage Index, as appropriate—to the unadjusted spending for services within each episode. To control for differences in the demographics and health status of enrollees in each MSA, we used a regression-based approach with enrollee-level variables such as age, gender, number of readmissions, and certain comorbidities. See app. I for a description of our approach.

[13] Examples of postdischarge services are services at a skilled nursing facility and home health services. Professional services include office visits, hospital consultations, surgeries, and other services provided by a physician or other health professional, such as a physician assistant. Examples of ancillary services are lab tests and ambulance services.

[14] We calculated volume, intensity, and price for hospital outpatient services but did not report them because we found that hospital outpatient spending constituted only 1 to 2 percent of episode spending. We could not calculate consistent measures of volume, intensity, and price for postdischarge care and ancillary services because of the variability of services within these categories and the absence of a measure of intensity for these services.

[15] Medicare bases its payment rates for physician services on RVUs, which reflect estimates of the resources needed to provide a given service relative to other services— including physician time and intensity; other clinical labor, equipment, and supplies; and premiums paid for malpractice.

[16] We did not report the names of certain MSAs to protect the confidentiality of entities contributing private data to the MarketScan database.

[17] See Institute of Medicine, *Variation in Health Care Spending: Target Decision Making, Not Geography* (Washington, D.C.: The National Academies Press, July 24, 2013). Health status was accounted for by IOM using diagnosis information recorded on claims; insurance plan factors included measures such as benefit generosity and plan type; and market-level factors included measures such as hospital competition, payer mix, and percentage of population uninsured.

[18] To do this work, IOM commissioned original analyses of public and private payer databases, and focused on describing and accounting for geographic variation in health care spending, utilization, and quality for the overall population, as well as for populations with specific diseases or conditions. IOM contractors quantified geographic variation in spending, utilization, and quality across various populations, payers, and geographic units; identified types of health care services with disproportionately high rates of variation; and identified

factors that drove variation, such as enrollee health status and demographic characteristics, health plan, and price and market factors, among other things.

[19] Medicare Payment Advisory Commission, "Chapter 7, Variation in private-sector payment rates," in *Report to the Congress: Medicare and the Health Care Delivery System* (June 15, 2011).

[20] GAO, *Federal Employees Health Benefits Program: Competition and Other Factors Linked to Wide Variation in Health Care Prices*, GAO-05-856 (Washington, D.C.: Aug. 15, 2005).

[21] These findings appear in a subcontractor report commissioned by IOM. See Michael McKellar et al., *Geographic Variation in Health Care Spending, Utilization, and Quality among the Privately Insured*, a special report prepared at the request of The Institute of Medicine Committee on Geographic Variation in Health Care Spending and Promotion of High-Value Care (Boston, Mass.: Harvard Medical School Department of Health Care Policy, Aug. 29, 2012).

[22] Chapin White, James D. Reschovsky, and Amelia M. Bond, *Inpatient Hospital Prices Drive Spending Variation for Episodes of Care for Privately Insured Patients*, Brief No. 14 (Washington, D.C.: National Institute for Health Care Reform, February 2014).

[23] The markets in this analysis included Louisville, Kentucky; Cleveland, Ohio; Lansing, Michigan; Flint, Michigan; Warren, Michigan; Detroit, Michigan; Kansas City, Missouri; Indianapolis, Indiana; and Buffalo, New York.

[24] The National Institute for Health Care Reform study included nine areas. IOM also reported less geographic variation in private sector spending per enrollee compared to our episode spending. Our study, with its focus on three hospital-based, surgical episodes of care, likely had a different composition of utilization of services (mix, quantity, and intensity) and prices, compared to the IOM's measure of total spending since not all services provided in medical practices are associated with inpatient admissions or surgical procedures.

[25] The correlation coefficient captures the relationship between two variables of interest and takes a value between negative 1 and 1. A correlation coefficient of 0 would indicate that there was no relationship between the variables. A correlation coefficient close to 1 would indicate a strong positive relationship, while a correlation coefficient close to negative 1 would indicate a strong negative relationship.

[26] Researchers at the National Institute for Health Care Reform found a correlation of 0.68 when comparing hospitals' spending on knee and hip replacements to spending across all types of episodes, and found a correlation of 0.80 when comparing cardiology episodes to all episodes. They concluded that a high-spending hospital for one episode type is also likely to have high spending for other episode types. IOM also studied this issue by conducting an episode-based analysis on a subset of conditions and, although finding correlation, the extent of the correlation depended on conditions examined. For example, the correlation between episode spending for diabetes and coronary heart disease was 0.79, but the correlation between spending on stroke and prostate cancer was 0.29.

[27] In addition, we examined whether the number of episodes in an MSA had an effect on average episode spending for that MSA, and did not find evidence of an effect.

[28] We identified price as the amount spent on the initial hospital inpatient admission (which excluded spending on any subsequent readmissions), because hospitals are generally paid one amount per admission regardless of the patient's length of stay or the services delivered.

[29] There was little or no difference across MSAs in the number of days in the initial admission. The average number of days was 2.32 in the lowest-spending quintile and 2.31 in the highest-spending quintile for coronary stent placement, 1.71 and 1.53 for laparoscopic appendectomy, and 2.87 and 2.91 for total hip replacement. Hospital inpatient prices generally cover all hospital services during an inpatient admission regardless of the length of stay or the services delivered, so there is no financial incentive for hospitals to keep patients for additional days in an inpatient setting.

[30] MSAs in the lowest- or highest-spending quintiles did not necessarily have spending on professional services that coincided with these quintiles. For example, for each of the three

procedures, San Jose, California, had a level of spending on professional services that was among the 10 highest-spending MSAs, even though it was not in the highest- spending quintile for episode spending for any procedure. In contrast, Madison, Wisconsin, had the highest or second-highest level of spending on professional services for all three procedures and was also in the highest-spending quintile for episode spending for all three procedures.

[31] Coronary stent placement, also known as percutaneous transluminal coronary angioplasty, is a surgical cardiology procedure to open a blocked coronary artery and insert a stent (an expandable metal coil) into the newly opened artery to help prevent renarrowing or reclosure. Laparoscopic appendectomy is a general surgical procedure to remove an infected appendix using instruments placed into small abdominal incisions. Total hip replacement, also known as total hip arthroplasty, is a surgical orthopedic procedure where cartilage and bone from the hip joint are replaced with prosthetic components.

[32] The MarketScan database contains claims for over 50 million enrollees paid by over 100 private insurers across 50 states and the District of Columbia in 2009 and 2010.

[33] For coronary stent placement, we identified enrollees with claims with a principal hospital procedure code for percutaneous transluminal coronary angioplasty or for coronary atherectomy and a professional procedure code for inserting an intracoronary stent, and we excluded enrollees with claims that indicated placement of a stent in more than one artery. For laparoscopic appendectomy, we identified enrollees with a principal hospital procedure code and a professional procedure code for laparoscopic appendectomy, and we excluded enrollees with claims that indicated extra work or additional procedures. For total hip replacement, we identified enrollees with claims with a principal hospital procedure code for total hip replacement and a professional procedure code for total hip arthroplasty, and we excluded enrollees with claims that indicated bilateral procedures.

[34] These procedures also have high levels of volume among all patients. For example, according to the Healthcare Cost and Utilization Project, which includes data for all privately insured, Medicare, Medicaid, uninsured, and all other patients, these 3 procedures were among the 20 procedures with the most discharges in 2009. During that year, there were approximately 614,000 discharges for coronary stent placement, approximately 200,000 discharges for laparoscopic appendectomy, and approximately 274,000 discharges for total hip replacement.

[35] In 2012, about one-third of all health care spending in the United States was for hospital services. Spending for professional services represented over one-quarter of spending, and the remainder of spending included services such as prescription drugs, nursing home care, and home health care, as well as administrative costs. See Centers for Medicare & Medicaid Services, *Table 2: National Health Expenditures; Aggregate and Per Capita Amounts, Annual Percent Change and Percent Distribution, by Type of Expenditure: Selected Calendar Years 1960-2012*, accessed October 28, 2014, http://www.cms.gov/Research-Statistics-Data-and-Systems/Statistics-Trends-and-Reports/NationalHealthExpendData/Downloads/tables.pdf.

[36] We excluded enrollees who had secondary insurance or were enrolled in a managed care or other capitated care plan because the claims data may not provide a complete record of all the services and spending associated with an episode of care.

[37] The Office of Management and Budget defines MSAs as having at least one urbanized area with a population of 50,000 or more, plus adjacent territory that has a high degree of social and economic integration with the core. Office of Management and Budget, Executive Office of the President, OMB Bulletin No. 13-01, *Revised Delineations of Metropolitan Statistical Areas, Micropolitan Statistical Areas, and Combined Statistical Areas, and Guidance on Uses of the Delineations of These Areas* (Washington, D.C.: Feb. 28, 2013).

[38] Before assigning episodes to MSAs, we excluded episodes with total spending that was three standard deviations above or below the national average of the lognormal distribution. After assigning episodes to MSAs, we excluded MSAs with less than 40 percent of episodes in either 2009 or 2010. We also excluded MSAs that had fewer than 24 coronary stent

placement episodes, fewer than 17 laparoscopic appendectomy episodes, or fewer than 24 total hip replacement episodes. We established these thresholds by sequentially dropping the MSA with the fewest episodes and analyzing the change in the national coefficient of variation of average episode spending for the remaining MSAs. The threshold for each procedure was based on the point at which the change in national coefficient of variation stabilized.

[39] We included any out-of-network claims because these claims are part of total spending by both the insurer and the enrollee on the episode. Therefore, to the extent that an insurer paid a higher rate to a non-network provider, we included those higher payments in our data. However, we did not include any balance billing because the MarketScan database does not include information on the billed charges.

[40] The correlation coefficient captures the relationship between two variables of interest and takes a value between negative 1 and 1. A correlation coefficient of 0 would indicate that there was no relationship between the variables. A correlation coefficient close to 1 would indicate a strong positive relationship, while a correlation coefficient close to negative 1 would indicate a strong negative relationship.

[41] Examples of postdischarge services are services at a skilled nursing facility and home health services. Professional services include office visits; hospital consultations; surgeries; and other services provided by a physician or other health professional, such as a physician assistant. Examples of ancillary services are lab tests and ambulance services.

[42] Although we compared MSAs in the lowest- and highest-spending quintiles for each procedure, we determined that our overall results would be similar if we compared MSAs based on the bottom and top 10th, 15th, or 25th percentile.

[43] We calculated volume, intensity, and price for hospital outpatient services but did not report them because we found that hospital outpatient spending constituted only 1 to 2 percent of episode spending. We could not calculate consistent measures of volume, intensity, and price for postdischarge care and ancillary services because of the variability of services within these categories and the absence of a measure of intensity for these services.

[44] Medicare bases its payment rates for physician services on RVUs, which reflect estimates of the resources needed to provide a given service relative to other services— including physician time and intensity; other clinical labor, rent, equipment, and supplies; and premiums paid for malpractice.

[45] We did not include volume for anesthesia services, which are measured in units of time and not the number of services. We also did not include intensity for anesthesia services, which are not assigned RVUs.

In: Geographic Variation …
Editor: Derrick Watkins

ISBN: 978-1-63482-875-8

Chapter 2

HEALTH INSURANCE: A PRIMER*

Bernadette Fernandez and Namrata K. Uberoi

SUMMARY

People obtain insurance to protect themselves against the possibility of financial loss in the future. Health insurance provides protection against the possibility of financial loss due to high health care expenses. Also, people do not know ahead of time exactly what their health care expenses will be, so paying for health insurance on a regular basis helps ease their out-of-pocket spending.

While health coverage continues to be mostly a private enterprise in this country, government plays an increasingly significant role. Government has initiated and responded to dynamics in medicine, the economy, and the workplace through legislation and public policies. One of the most recent efforts was enactment and ongoing implementation of the Patient Protection and Affordable Care Act (ACA; P.L. 111-148, as amended). ACA includes provisions to encourage the expansion of health insurance coverage, and establish new federal health insurance standards, among other reforms.

Americans obtain health insurance in different settings and through a variety of methods. In 2013, a majority (64.2%) of Americans obtained health insurance through the private sector, which includes both employer-sponsored and individual market coverage. Public programs

* This is an edited, reformatted and augmented version of a Congressional Research Service publication RL32237, prepared for Members and Committees of Congress dated January 8, 2015.

(Medicare, Medicaid/CHIP, or health services for military service members and veterans) provided coverage to 34.3% of Americans. Approximately 13.4% of Americans were uninsured for the entire year of 2013.

Health insurance benefits are delivered and financed under different systems. The factors that distinguish one delivery system from another are many, including how health care is financed, how much access to providers and services is controlled, and how much authority the enrollee has to design her/his health plan. To illustrate, managed care is characterized by predetermined restrictions on accessing services and providers, whereas individual decision-making regarding use of health benefits is a hallmark of consumer driven health care, such as health savings accounts. As economic conditions change, a specific delivery system may gain or lose the interest of affected parties.

INTRODUCTION

As health insurance coverage has evolved from an uncommon benefit to a routine one, government's role in subsidizing and regulating that coverage also has changed. While most insured Americans obtain health coverage through the private sector, public entities play an increasingly significant role.

The federal government's involvement in health coverage expanded dramatically over the past several decades:

- A long-standing rule issued by the Internal Revenue Service (IRS) in 1954 stated that an employer's contributions to employer-sponsored health insurance are not to be included in an employee's gross income for tax purposes (Internal Revenue Code, Section 106). This ruling helped spur the growth of employer-sponsored health benefits. The IRS also stated separately that employers could deduct such contributions as part of business expenses.
- Advances in medicine led to increased costs of treatment, which was especially problematic for certain groups of consumers who lacked health coverage. This led to government efforts to assist health care consumers in paying for medical services through the 1965 Medicare and Medicaid social insurance programs.[1]
- More and more employees began to work for more than one employer over their lifetimes. The federal government enacted the Health

Insurance Portability and Accountability Act of 1996 (HIPAA) to provide certain protections to workers that switched or lost jobs.

- In response to a persistent rate of uninsurance, the federal government in 2010 passed the Patient Protection and Affordable Care Act (ACA; P.L. 111-148, as amended), which instituted a large set of reforms to the private insurance market and expanded publicly funded coverage.

Given the frequent introduction of legislation aimed at modifying or building on the current health insurance system, understanding the potential impact of such proposals requires a working knowledge of how health insurance is provided, purchased, and regulated. This report provides background information about these topics.

WHAT IS HEALTH INSURANCE?

Definitions and Principles

People buy insurance to protect themselves against the possibility of financial loss in the future. Such losses may be due to a motor vehicle collision, natural disaster, or other circumstance. For individuals, financial losses may result from the substantial[2] use of health care services. Health insurance provides protection against the possibility of financial loss due to high health care expenses. Also, people do not know ahead of time exactly what their health care expenses will be, so paying for health insurance on a regular basis helps to smooth out their spending.

The concept underlying insurance is *risk* (i.e., the likelihood and magnitude of financial loss). In any type of insurance arrangement, all parties seek to minimize their own risk. In health insurance, consumers and insurers approach the management of insurance risk differently. From the consumer's point of view, a person (or family) buys health insurance to protect against financial losses resulting from the future use of medical care. From the insurer's point of view, it employs a variety of methods to manage the risk it takes on when providing health coverage to consumers, to assure that it operates a profitable business.[3] One method is to charge higher premiums for older consumers (to the extent allowed under federal law), because medical expenses tend to increase with age. While the methods employed by an insurer differ from those of a consumer, each has the same goal: to minimize risk in an uncertain future. It is this uncertainty of the future and risk of financial loss which form the context for insurance, and the strategies to make financial loss more predictable and manageable which drive insurance arrangements.

Risk Pools

A function of insurance is to spread risk across a group of people. This is achieved in health insurance when people contribute to a common pool (*risk pool*) an amount at least equal to the *expected* cost resulting from use of covered services by the group as a whole. In this way, the *actual* costs of health services used by a few people are spread over the entire group. This is the reason why insuring larger groups is considered less risky—the more individuals participating in a risk pool, the less likely that the serious medical experiences of one or a few persons will result in catastrophic financial loss for the entire pool.

An insurer calculates and charges a premium in order to finance the health coverage it provides. The premium reflects several components, including the expected cost of claims for health care use in a year, administrative expenses associated with running the plan, and a profit margin.[4] If the insurer accurately estimates future costs and sets appropriate premium levels for all enrollees, then that risk pool has reached equilibrium. This equilibrium is often achieved by healthy persons in the risk pool helping to subsidize the higher-than-average costs of less-healthy persons in the pool.

This redistributive effect is a primary feature of insurance, because it is generally understood that a minority of consumers is responsible for a majority of expenses. According to an analysis of national health care expenditure data, the top 5% of the population accounted for nearly half of all health expenditures in 2011 and 2012.[5] Because of this uneven distribution of expenses, in a risk pool it would be expected that costs attributed to those who incur the greatest expenses would be spread across the pool.

Risk Pool Composition and Adverse Selection

As noted above, one of the ways insurers attempt to make future costs more predictable is by spreading the risk of a few high-cost individuals across many people. But the number of people in a risk pool is not the only significant factor. Equally as important, if not more so, is the composition of the group.

A consumer's intention to obtain health coverage is based on a variety of factors, such as individual health status, estimated need for future medical care, and disposable income. Consumers with different health conditions, as well as varying degrees of comfort towards risk-taking, will differ on whether they consider health insurance necessary. However, with many companies offering their workers an employer subsidy for insurance plans, even those unlikely to incur significant medical expenses are incentivized to obtain coverage under this arrangement, if it is available to them. Because consumers are required by law (with certain individuals excepted) to either obtain insurance or face a penalty, their willingness to pay this penalty will also factor into their decision.[6]

Individuals who expect or plan for high use of health services tend to enroll in more generous (and consequently more expensive) health plans, a phenomenon known as *adverse selection*. An extreme example of adverse selection is when a disproportionate share of unhealthy people makes up a risk pool and the cost for each person in the pool rises. The higher costs may encourage the departure of healthier members and discourage the entrance of other healthy people, since healthier people may be able to find cheaper coverage elsewhere or decide that coverage is too costly and become uninsured (and pay a penalty). In either situation, it leaves an even less healthy group of people in the risk pool, which again causes the cost to rise for the remaining participants. If there is no change in this dynamic, the group may experience a self-reinforcing rise in costs as it suffers substantial adverse selection, leading to an increasingly expensive risk pool and possibly dissolution of the pool altogether.

Group and Nongroup Market

Health insurance can be provided to groups of people that are drawn together by an employer or other organization, such as a union. Such groups are generally formed for some purpose other than obtaining insurance, like employment. When insurance is provided to a group, it is referred to as *group coverage* or *group insurance*. In the group market, the entity that provides health benefits to the group (e.g., an employer) is referred to as the plan *sponsor*.

The group insurance market is divided into two segments, small group and large group, defined by the size of the employer or other organization purchasing a group insurance plan. Since some ACA reforms focus specifically on the small group insurance market, it is important to note the distinction in size between the small and large group markets. Before enactment of the ACA, the dividing line between small and large groups was typically 50 employees. In 2016, the dividing line will increase to 100 employees. Thus businesses with fewer than 100 employees will be defined as *small employers* and be eligible for small group coverage. Until the 100 employee large group definition takes effect in 2016, ACA allows states to choose whether to define *small employers* as those that employ 100 or fewer employees or those that employ 50 or fewer employees.[7]

Consumers who are not associated with a group can obtain health coverage by purchasing it directly from an insurer in the nongroup (*individual*) insurance market. The individual market enrolls many people who do not receive coverage from an employer—those who are self-employed, unemployed, or work part-time, and who are otherwise ineligible for public insurance programs like Medicare or Medicaid.

Fully Insured vs. Self-Insured Plans

A common distinction made between types of group health insurance products is whether they are fully insured or self-insured. A fully insured health plan is one in which the plan sponsor purchases health coverage from a state-licensed insurance carrier. The carrier assumes the risk of providing health benefits to the sponsor's enrolled members and the individuals/families directly purchasing individual insurance policies. In contrast, organizations that self-insure (or self-fund) do not purchase health coverage from insurers. Self-insured plans refer to health coverage that is provided directly by the organization seeking coverage for its members (e.g., a firm providing health benefits to its employees). Such organizations set aside funds and pay for health benefits directly. Under self-insurance, the organization bears the risk for covering medical expenses, and such benefit plans are not subject to state insurance regulations.8 Firms that self-insure may contract with third-party administrators (TPAs) to handle administrative duties such as member services, premium collection, and utilization review. TPAs do not underwrite insurance risk.

Self-Only vs. Family Coverage

Another common distinction made in health insurance refers to the scope of coverage provided under a health plan; that is, whether the coverage is for one person, a family, or other groupings. Under self-only coverage, the holder of the insurance policy is the only person insured. (Self-only coverage is also called individual coverage. Individual coverage in this sense should not be confused with health coverage from the individual insurance market—see discussion above.) Family coverage applies to the policyholder and his or her dependents. Other coverage arrangements may include self plus one, and self plus children.

Tax Exclusion for Employer-Sponsored Insurance

Health insurance coverage in the United States is delivered through a patchwork approach, which includes private and public sources, of providing and paying for health insurance and health care.

One of the key pieces of this approach encouraged the growth of employer-sponsored health coverage via the tax code.[9]

Section 106 of the Internal Revenue Code states that employer contributions to employer-sponsored health insurance are not included in workers' gross incomes for tax purposes. This tax preference encourages workers to sign up for (*take-up*) health coverage within the work setting. Moreover, employers' premium contributions are excluded from wages for the purpose of calculating employment taxes, which include Social Security and Medicare taxes, and unemployment taxes.[10] Exclusion of these contributions directly affects the amounts that employers and workers pay in taxes. In addition to the tax advantages, employer-sponsored health coverage allows both parties to benefit in other ways: employers use health insurance coverage as a means to recruit and retain workers, while workers have traditionally gained access to more plan choices at better rates than those seeking nongroup insurance (see discussion below). However, economic theory suggests that workers receive reduced wages to compensate for richer benefits.

The tax exclusion of health benefits is one of the primary reasons why health insurance coverage is provided mainly through the workplace in the United States. For example, approximately 53.9% of Americans had employer-sponsored insurance in 2013.[11] Furthermore, the tax exclusion of employer-sponsored insurance is the largest single tax expenditure by the federal government. The Congressional Budget Office estimated that the employer-sponsored health insurance exclusion from both income and payroll taxes would cost the government $248 billion in 2013.[12]

Health Insurance Premiums

A person enrolled in a private health insurance plan must pay a fee (*premium*), typically on a monthly basis, to maintain coverage under the plan. An insurer will then pay for a certain proportion of health care services and items at the time they are received (after the plan's deductible is met, if applicable), with the enrollee paying the rest of the cost out of pocket, an arrangement known as cost-sharing.

Premiums are used for three general purposes: payments for medical claims, administrative costs, and a profit margin. Claims payments make up the largest component of premiums, ranging from 85% to 88% of fully insured plans between 2006 and 2011.[13] The magnitude of claims payments is a function of both the *quantity* of health services (e.g., hospital visits) and items (e.g., prescription drugs) used and the *price* for each corresponding service and item (less any applicable enrollee cost-sharing), with rising prices, not quantity, generally being the main driver of total payments.[14] Administrative costs and a relatively modest profit margin—less than 5% in recent years[15]—make up the rest of premiums.

Premiums for U.S. insurance plans are difficult to summarize not only because plans can be arranged on behalf of a group by an organization such as an employer or purchased individually under a different set of regulations, but also because plans can cover a single person (self-only coverage), an entire family, or some combination in between. In addition, reliable premium information, especially for the nongroup market, can be difficult to find. Also, comparing premiums between groups is difficult considering the products (i.e., insurance) varies.

An annual source of employer health benefits data found that the average annual premium for self-only coverage was $6,025 in 2014. The average premium for a family of four was $16,834 that same year.[16] For self-only coverage, the cost of employer-sponsored health benefits was similar to the prior year. Compared to the previous year's average premiums, the cost for employer-sponsored health benefits for family coverage increased 3%. While this signals a reprieve from the double-digit increases that have occurred in the past, average premium growth rates still outpaced both wage growth and general inflation.[17]

Nongroup premiums have also risen in recent years. For instance, the individual market saw its national average rate of premium increase grow from 9.9% to 11.7% between 2008 and 2010.[18]

Administrative Expenses

Health insurance companies are complex organizations requiring specialized expertise and technology to develop, market, and operate a health plan. Administrative expenses include costs associated with contracting with providers, sales and marketing, enrollment and billing, customer service, utilization review, case management, and other functions. Given that administration is an essential component of an insurer's business, such expenses comprise an integral component of premiums.

Insurance companies report administrative costs in regulatory filings to applicable state entities. Such data indicate a relatively stable trend. From 2009 to 2013, general administrative expenses and claims adjustment expenses together took up between 11.7% and 12.1% of health insurers' net written premiums.[19]

Regulation of Health Insurance

Health insurance regulation addresses a wide variety of issues: the benefits that must be offered, the individuals to whom the insurance is made available, and the responsibilities insurers have to consumers, to name a few. One of the most enduring issues regarding health insurance regulation is whether it is the responsibility of individual states or the federal government.

Primary Responsibility of the States

The regulation of insurance traditionally has been a state responsibility, as clarified by the 1945 McCarran-Ferguson Act. Individual states have established standards and regulations overseeing the *business of insurance*, including requirements related to the finances, management, and business practices of an insurer. For example, all states have laws that require state-licensed insurance carriers to offer coverage for specified health services (*benefit mandates* or *mandated benefits*). Because fully-insured plans are subject to state-established requirements, those plans must offer those mandated benefits. On the other hand, self-insured plans are not subject to state insurance regulations so they are exempt from such requirements.

Key Federal Laws

Despite the states' role as the primary regulators of health insurance, overlapping federal requirements complicate regulation of the health insurance industry. Three federal laws in particular—the Employee Retirement Income Security Act of 1974 (ERISA; P.L. 93-406), the Health Insurance Portability and Accountability Act of 1996 (HIPAA; P.L. 104-191), and the Patient Protection and Affordable Care Act (ACA; P.L. 111-148, as amended)—have a significant impact on how private health insurance is provided.

ERISA outlines minimum federal standards for private-sector employer-sponsored benefits. (Public employee benefits and plans sponsored by churches are exempt from ERISA). Passed in response to abuses in the private pension system, the Act was developed with a focus on pensions but the law applies to a long list of *welfare benefits*, including health benefits. ERISA requires that funds be handled prudently and in the best interest of beneficiaries, participants be informed of their rights, and there be adequate disclosure of a plan's financial activities. It preempts state laws that *relate to* employee benefit plans. (In other words, the federal law overrides state laws affecting private-sector employee benefits.) This portion of ERISA was designed to ensure that plans would be subject to the same benefit laws across all states, partly in consideration of firms that operate in multiple states. However, state laws still apply for issues which involve the *business of insurance*. The delineation of issues attributable to the phrases *relate to* and *business of insurance* is not clear, and has led to long-standing debates and active litigation over the scope of ERISA preemption.[20]

The core motivation behind the Health Insurance Portability and Accountability Act of 1996 (HIPAA) was to address the concern that insured persons had about losing their coverage if they switched jobs or changed health plans (*portability* of health coverage). The Act's health insurance provisions established federal requirements for private and public employer-sponsored health plans and insurers. These requirements included

- ensuring the availability and renewability of coverage for certain employees and other persons under specified circumstances,
- limiting the amount of time that coverage for preexisting medical conditions can be excluded, and
- prohibiting discrimination on the basis of health status-related factors.

The Act also includes tax provisions designed to encourage the expansion of health coverage through several mechanisms, such as authorizing tax-advantaged medical savings accounts, and a graduated increase of the portion of premiums self-employed persons may deduct from their federal income tax calculations.[21] Another set of HIPAA provisions addresses the electronic transmission of health information and the privacy of personally identifiable medical information (administrative simplification and privacy provisions, respectively).[22]

The 111th Congress passed comprehensive health reform legislation: the Patient Protection and Affordable Care Act (ACA; P.L. 111-148, as amended).[23] Enacted on March 23, 2010, and subsequently amended by a number of laws (including the Health Care and Education Affordability

Reconciliation Act of 2010; P.L. 111-152), ACA includes private insurance provisions that impose new requirements on individuals,[24] employers,[25] and health plans;[26] and provides financial assistance to certain individuals[27] and, in some cases, small employers.[28] These provisions include market reforms that impose certain requirements on private insurance plans and sponsors of insurance; establish insurance exchanges (*marketplaces*) where individuals and small businesses[29] can shop for and purchase health plans that meet or exceed federal standards; provide subsidies to certain individuals purchasing insurance from an exchange; establish an individual mandate for most individuals to purchase insurance or pay a penalty; and assess penalties on certain employers that do not provide insurance for their employees that meets preset standards of affordability and value.

SOURCES OF HEALTH INSURANCE

Americans obtain health insurance through a variety of methods and from different sources (see *Figure 1*). People may get it through the private sector or from a government source. Consumers may purchase health coverage on their own, as part of an employee group, or through a trade or professional association. Individuals can also have multiple sources of coverage in a year. That is, they may have multiple types of coverage at one time or even switch coverage types within a year.[30] This report discusses health insurance coverage in three categories: (1) insured through private sources, [31] (2) coverage under public programs,[32] or (3) uninsured.

Private Insurance

Private insurance, which includes both employer-sponsored (*group market*) and individual market (*nongroup*) coverage, accounts for the substantial majority of Americans with health insurance. In 2013, approximately 201 million individuals (64.2% of the U.S. population) received coverage through private insurance.[33]

The ACA introduced a number of significant reforms to the private insurance market, mostly directed to the individual and small group markets. Collectively, ACA's market reforms have substantially altered the landscape for private insurance.

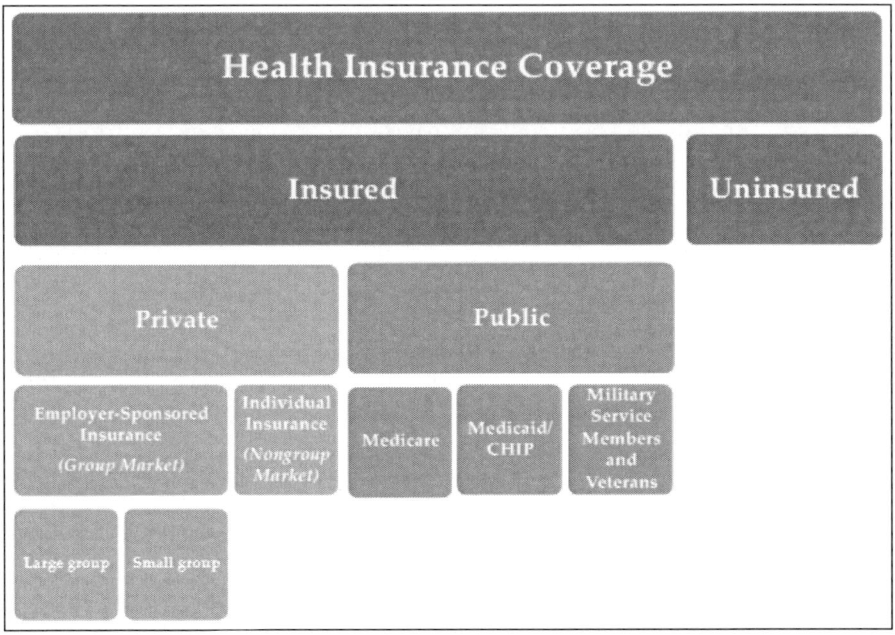

Source: Congressional Research Service (CRS) illustration of sources of health insurance coverage.

Notes: This figure is not drawn to scale; it is an illustration of the sources of health insurance and does not reflect their relative sizes.

Figure 1. Sources of Health Insurance.

Employer-Sponsored Insurance

Group health insurance is typically offered by employers, and most Americans obtain health coverage through the workplace. In 2013, approximately 169 million persons had employer-sponsored health insurance (ESI), which accounts for approximately 53.9% of the total U.S. population.[34]

Under ESI, risk pools may be comprised of active workers, dependents, and retirees. Insurers use a number of strategies to increase the likelihood that each risk pool includes a good proportion of healthy individuals. For instance, insurers may restrict employees' opportunities to take up health coverage or switch health plans by designating a specific time frame each year for such activities (*open enrollment period*). This strategy decreases the likelihood that people will *game* the system by taking up coverage only when they plan on using health services (e.g., for pregnancy and childbirth), and dropping coverage when they no longer plan to access care.[35] Employers also use strategies to encourage insurance take-up by healthy people. For example, employers typically make contributions that cover most of the health insurance premium. In 2014, employers paid more than 80% of the total premium amounts for self-only plans and more than 70% for family plans, on average.[36] This subsidy makes health coverage a more attractive benefit, even to those workers who do not plan to use medical services on a regular basis. By encouraging healthy workers to take-up health insurance, the employer subsidy helps to avoid adverse selection and contributes to the stability and diversity of the risk pool.

ESI has a number of strengths from the worker perspective. The employer premium contribution is exempt from individual income taxes, so workers are given a tax advantage by purchasing coverage through an employer compared with the individual insurance (*nongroup*) market. In addition, employer-sponsored coverage typically is heavily subsidized, so workers generally do not directly bear the full cost of insurance. Both the tax advantages and employer subsidy encourage the growth and continuity of ESI, historically providing an advantage over the individual market.[37]

For plan sponsors, health benefits are a common component of employee compensation used toward the recruitment and retention of workers. In addition, employers' premium contributions are excluded from wages for the purpose of calculating employment taxes, which directly affects the taxes owed by employers (and workers). Moreover, large employers that offer health coverage that meets certain standards will have complied with the ACA employer requirements, thus avoiding the employer tax for noncompliance.[38] Finally, certain small employers are eligible for small business tax credits if they contribute at least half of their employees' health insurance costs.[39]

While there are many advantages to obtaining ESI coverage, there are challenges as well. From the vantage point of the enrollee, one of the biggest disadvantages is the general lack of portability. Because ESI coverage is tied to the job and not the person, a change in employment (such as going from full-time to part-time status, or changing jobs) may alter the health care providers or services to which the worker has access, or disrupt health coverage altogether. Also, in firms that offer health coverage, there is a trade-off made between wages and benefits. For workers who do not take up health insurance from those firms, they end up accepting lower wages for a set of benefits they do not use. From the perspective of the plan sponsor, an underlying challenge is the lack of enrollee awareness of the true costs of health care. Because the sponsor usually contributes to the cost of the premium, enrollees do not bear the full cost of obtaining health coverage. Given this lack of awareness regarding total costs, sponsors' efforts to constrain their own health spending—by increasing the employee share of the premium or costsharing—are made even more difficult to justify or implement. Finally, from the perspective of the federal budget, the tax exclusion of employer-sponsored health insurance represents the largest source of foregone revenue.

Individual Health Insurance

The individual insurance (*nongroup*) market is referred to as a *residual* market, because it provides coverage to those who either cannot obtain health insurance through the workplace (i.e., employer-sponsored insurance) or do not qualify for public programs like Medicare, Medicaid, or the State Children's Health Insurance Program (CHIP). The residual nature of the individual insurance market is reflected in the demographic make-up of those who purchase coverage from it: many individuals with nongroup insurance are part-time workers, part-year workers, and self-employed persons—individuals who are unlikely to have access to employer coverage. In addition, some people use the individual insurance market as a temporary source of coverage, such as those in-between jobs or early retirees who are not yet eligible for Medicare.[40] The enrollee population of the market has also historically been small, with just 11% of the U.S. population covered by insurance purchased from the individual market in 2013.[41]

The insurance market reforms in the ACA specifically target the individual insurance market (as well as the small group market), in large part because the individual market lacked the advantages and protections compared with the large group market. Prior to ACA, individuals could be denied insurance altogether, charged a higher premium because of individual characteristics, and face benefit exclusions based on preexisting health conditions (if allowed under state law). State law varied greatly in terms of patient protections. ACA's market reforms and exchange provisions, which build on an existing but limited federal floor of insurance standards, affect the offer, issuance, generosity, and pricing of health plans, among other issues.[42] For example, ACA established a new tax credit that qualified individuals and families may use toward the purchase of insurance through exchanges.[43] Collectively, the market reforms and exchanges have transformed the plans and carrier practices in the individual insurance market, and standardized (to some degree) the patchwork of health regulation across the country.[44]

The ACA requires the establishment of a health insurance exchange in every state. ACA exchanges are marketplaces where individuals and small businesses can shop for and purchase private health insurance. The exchanges are intended to simplify the health insurance purchasing process and assist individuals in shopping for qualified health plans, applying for premium subsidies, enrolling in individual health plans, and even determining whether they qualify for Medicaid or other government programs. States can choose to run their own exchange, opt for a state-federal partnership, or have a federally facilitated exchange.[45]

Enrollment in the individual insurance market overall may increase due to ACA's market reforms, health insurance exchanges, and tax credits. The Congressional Budget Office and Joint Committee on Taxation project that by 2024, 25 million people under age 65 will be covered by nongroup insurance purchased from exchanges, representing a net increase in nongroup coverage of about 20 million.[46]

Public Programs

While most Americans with health insurance obtain it through the private sector, 107.6 million (34.3% of the U.S. population) people got health coverage through programs administered by the government in 2013.[47] Below are descriptions of selected public programs which provide health insurance coverage to eligible persons.

Medicare

In 2013, almost 49 million (15.6% of the U.S. population) individuals obtained coverage through Medicare.[48] The Medicare program was established in 1965, and is a federal program for persons age 65 and older and certain persons with disabilities. Medicare consists of four parts: Part A, Hospital Insurance; Part B, Supplementary Medical Insurance; Part C, Medicare Advantage; and Part D, the prescription drug benefit. The Medicare program provides coverage for a wide range of medical services, such as care provided in hospitals and skilled nursing facilities, hospice care, home health care, physician services, physical and occupational therapy, outpatient prescription drug benefits, and other services. Medicare has been so successful in covering the elderly that the problem of uninsurance usually is described in terms of the under-65 population.[49]

Medicaid and the State Children's Health Insurance Program

Medicaid covered approximately 54.1 million people (17.3% of the U.S. population) in 2013.[50] Medicaid is a joint federal and state program that finances the delivery of health care services to millions of low-income Americans. It is a means-tested program, and applicants must meet financial and other criteria in order to be eligible for services. Everyone who meets the eligibility criteria is entitled to Medicaid benefits available in their state of residence. Medicaid provides coverage for health care including primary and acute care as well as long-term services and supports to certain low-income adults, children, the elderly, and persons with disabilities. It is jointly funded by federal and state governments, and is administered by the states within federal guidelines. State Medicaid programs generally provide a comprehensive set of services, reflecting their diverse enrollee population. These programs must provide a set of federally-specified benefits for qualified individuals, such as hospital services (both inpatient and outpatient), physician services, nursing home care for individuals aged 21 and over, home health care, and certain services for children. States may also cover additional *optional services* and beneficiaries. Some states have used waiver authority under Medicaid to extend coverage to uninsured persons who do not meet the program's categorical and/or financial tests.[51] ACA includes provisions that significantly expand eligibility for Medicaid beginning in 2014, although individual states can elect not to participate in this expansion.[52]

The State Children's Health Insurance Program was established in 1997 to provide health coverage to uninsured low-income children who are ineligible for Medicaid. In designing their programs, states can choose among three options: expand Medicaid, create a separate CHIP program, or adopt a combination of both approaches. States that choose to expand Medicaid to CHIP eligibles must provide the full range of mandatory Medicaid benefits, as well as all optional services specified in their state Medicaid plans. States that establish CHIP programs that are separate from Medicaid choose one of three benefit options. All 50 states, the District of Columbia, and five territories have established some type of CHIP program. CHIP's eligibility rules target uninsured children under 19 years of age whose families' incomes are above Medicaid eligibility levels.[53]

Military Service Members and Veterans

In 2013, approximately 14.1 million persons (4.5% of the U.S. population) were covered by health care services for military service members and veterans.[54] Health care services for military service members and veterans are provided by the Department of Defense (DOD) through TRICARE or by the Department of Veterans Affairs (VA) through the VA system and the Civilian Health and Medical Program of the Department of Veterans Affairs (CHAMPVA).

The DOD administers health care services through the TRICARE program to eligible beneficiaries that include active duty uniformed personnel, eligible members of the Reserve Component, uniformed services retirees; as well as their dependents and survivors. TRICARE is administered on a regional basis and provides health services through military and nonmilitary hospitals, clinics, and providers.[55]

The Department of Veterans Affairs, through the Veterans Health Administration, operates the nation's largest integrated direct health care delivery system. The VA system is a veteran-specific national health care system in which the federal government owns the medical facilities and employs the health care providers. VA health care eligibility is based on veteran status, presence of service-connected disabilities or exposures, income, and/ or other factors.[56] Unlike TRICARE, VA health care covers a select group of dependents through CHAMPVA.[57]

The Uninsured

Despite the multiple sources of public and private health insurance coverage, millions of Americans are without health coverage. In 2013, approximately 42 million people (13.4% of the U.S. population) were without coverage.[58] For the vast majority of the uninsured, they lack coverage because they cannot *access* coverage (e.g., their employer does not offer health insurance as an employment benefit) or they cannot *afford* it.

Uninsurance is characterized as a problem of the under-65 population, given near-universal coverage of seniors through Medicare. One of the most striking characteristics of persons who lack coverage is that a significant proportion are in low-income families. For instance, among all uninsured persons under age 65, well over half were in poor or near-poor families in 2012.[59]

A defining characteristic of the nonelderly uninsured population is that most have ties to the paid labor force. In 2012, "just over 80 percent of the uninsured lived in families headed by workers."[60] While such findings may be counter-intuitive, there are multiple reasons why employed persons and their families may lack health coverage. For example, a worker may be offered health insurance by his/her employer, but declines it because he/she thinks it is too expensive. An employee may work for a small firm which is less likely than a large firm to offer health insurance as a benefit. Finally, a healthy worker may be willing to take on the risk of being uninsured and choose not to purchase insurance at all. So, despite the dominance of employer-sponsored health insurance, the dynamics of employment status, health conditions, and financial resources intersect to historically impede coverage of all workers and their families.

Consequences of Uninsurance

While health insurance coverage is not necessary to obtain health care, it is a useful mechanism for accessing services in an environment of increasingly expensive health care. As health care costs continue to rise, more people need greater assistance with covering medical expenses. Health insurance provides some measure of protection for consumers, especially for those who have limited means or greater-than-average need for medical care.

Health insurance is considered important also because of the well-documented, far-reaching consequences of uninsurance. For instance, uninsured persons are more likely to forgo needed health care than people with health coverage.[61] This includes forgoing services for preventable or chronic conditions, which often leads to worse health outcomes. Uninsured persons also are less likely to have a *usual source of care*, that is, a person or place identified as the source to which the consumer *usually* goes for health services or medical advice (not including emergency rooms). Having a usual source is important because people who establish ongoing relationships with health care providers or facilities are more likely to access preventive health services and have regular visits with a physician, compared with individuals without a usual source.[62]

The ACA now requires most individuals to maintain health insurance coverage for themselves and their dependents, or otherwise pay a penalty. Some individuals are exempt[63] from the individual mandate and the penalty. Individuals who do not maintain minimum essential coverage and are not exempt from the mandate will have to pay a penalty for each month of noncompliance. In 2014, the annual penalty was the greater of $95 or 1% of applicable income. In 2015, the annual penalty is the greater of $325 or 2% of applicable income.[64]

Expanding coverage is one of the primary objectives of the ACA. The Congressional Budget Office and the Joint Committee on Taxation estimated that ACA will increase the number of nonelderly Americans with health insurance by about 26 million by 2024 relative to the projected trend without ACA. The share of nonelderly U.S. residents with insurance coverage in 2024 is estimated to be around 89%, compared with a projected share of around 80% in the absence of the law. However, approximately 31 million nonelderly U.S. residents are estimated to remain uninsured, including individuals who choose not to purchase health insurance and are subject to the penalty for non-compliance to the ACA's individual mandate, individuals who are exempt from the individual mandate, and undocumented individuals.[65]

CONCLUSION

Health insurance in the United States is a patchwork comprised of a combination of private and government sources. In 2013, a majority (64.2%) of Americans obtained health insurance through the private sector, which includes both employer-sponsored and nongroup coverage. Public programs (Medicare, Medicaid/CHIP, or health care services for military service members and veterans) provided coverage to 34.3% of Americans. Approximately 13.4% of Americans were uninsured for the entire year of 2013.[66,67]

Within each of the sources, health insurance differs by the market structure itself—group versus nongroup, fully insured versus self-insured; self-only versus family coverage, etc. Overlaying this patchwork are also regulations from both the federal and state level. In addition, the ACA instituted a large set of reforms to the private insurance market and expanded publicly funded coverage. Health care is also delivered and financed through different arrangements (e.g., indemnity insurance, managed care, and consumer-driven health care), which are further discussed in the *Appendix*. The popularity of some of these mechanisms has also changed over time.

APPENDIX. HOW IS PRIVATE HEALTH COVERAGE PROVIDED?

Given the complexity of the health care system overall, it is no surprise that health coverage is delivered and financed through different arrangements. Those arrangements vary due to numerous factors such as how health care is financed, how much access to providers and services is controlled, and how much flexibility the enrollees have to use the services covered under her/his health plan. While delivery systems may share certain characteristics, general distinctions can be made based on payment, access, and other critical variables.

Indemnity Insurance

Under indemnity insurance, the insured person decides when and from whom to seek health services. If the services the enrollee receives are covered under his/her insurance, the enrollee or the enrollee's provider files a claim with the insurer. Thus, insurers make payments *retrospectively* (i.e., after the health services have been rendered), up to the maximum amounts specified for each covered service. In this model of health care delivery, the financing of health services and the obtaining of those services are kept separate.

This bifurcated arrangement was unquestioned for a time. But as medical costs began to rise, sometimes faster than other sectors of the national economy, many observers criticized this delivery model as contributing to increasing expenditures. Because providers were compensated on a fee-for-service basis, some argued that providers were not given incentives to provide efficient health care. In fact, some critics accused health care practitioners and institutions of providing an over-abundance of health care in order to generate greater revenue.[68] By the early 1970s, legislators, analysts, and others expressed considerable interest in alternative models, such as managed care models, with cost control as a key feature.

Managed Care

While managed care means different things to different people, several key characteristics set it apart from traditional (indemnity) insurance. One of the main differences is that the service delivery and financing functions are integrated under managed care. Managed care organizations (MCOs) employ various techniques to control costs and manage health service use *prospectively*. Among those techniques are restricting enrollee access to certain providers (*in-network* providers); requiring primary-care-physician approval for access to specialty care (*gatekeeping*); coordinating care for persons with certain conditions (*disease management* or *case management*); and requiring prior authorization for routine hospital inpatient care (*pre-*

certification). MCOs may offer different types of health plans that vary in the degree to which cost and medical decision-making is controlled. As a consequence, enrollee costs also vary. Generally, the more tightly managed a plan is, the lower the premium. Other distinguishing features of the managed care approach include an emphasis on preventive health care and implementation of quality assurance processes.

Managed care was touted as the antidote to rapidly rising health care costs. Starting with the passage of federal legislation in the 1970s which supported the growth of managed care (specifically in the form of health maintenance organizations (HMOs)), the number of MCOs grew quickly. Increased market competition among these organizations led to decreases in premiums, in order to gain market share. With high medical inflation in the 1980s and early 1990s, enrollees flocked to these less-costly managed care plans. By the mid-1990s, more insured workers were enrolled in HMOs than any other health plan type—contributing to the substantial displacement of traditional indemnity insurance[69]—and health insurance premiums had stabilized.[70]

But in the latter half of the 1990s, a *backlash* against managed care started to grow.[71] Some enrollees had grown weary of provider and service restrictions. Many MCOs that had increased market share through artificially low premiums began to raise them in order to increase revenue.[72] Consumers and others accused the managed care industry of caring more about controlling costs than providing health care.[73] Some providers resented the role managed care played in medical decision-making. Many enrollees began to leave HMOs. The industry responded by developing insurance products that were less-tightly managed, but more costly. Some traditional HMOs widened their provider networks and eliminated the gatekeeping function, while employers began to offer plan types that were less tightly managed, such as preferred provider organizations (PPOs).[74] In fact, by the end of the 1990s, more people with work-based health coverage were enrolled in PPOs than in HMOs.[75]

As the influence of managed care waned and health care costs began to rise at an increasing pace during the late 1990s, consumers began to feel the impact. For example, in the employment setting, employers absorbed the extra costs at first in order to recruit and retain workers during the booming economy of the mid to late 1990s.[76] But as the economy soured, employers began to pass these expenses along to enrollees by increasing employees' contributions to their own coverage.[77]

Consumer-Driven Health Care

By the end of the 1990s, large increases in health costs again became commonplace. With the belief by some observers that the age of managed care was over, they began to search for alternatives. Consumer-driven (or consumer-directed) health care has been offered as one such option.

Consumer-driven health care refers to a broad spectrum of coverage arrangements that give incentives to consumers to control their use of health services and/or ration their own health benefits. While consumer-driven health care can take on many forms, the premise common to all of these approaches is that by making enrollees more responsible for the cost of their own health care, it creates incentives for people to use services prudently. The expectation is that greater cost-consciousness on the part of consumers will result in lower overall health costs. In essence, the service and cost control functions administered by MCOs and providers under managed care shifts in part to enrollees under the consumer-driven health care model.

One example that is at the heart of discussions about consumer-driven care is the health savings account (HSA). An HSA, in and of itself, is not a health insurance plan. Instead, it is an investment account in which contributions earn interest tax free. Consumers, their employers, or both may make contributions to HSAs. Consumers withdraw funds on a tax-free basis to cover medical expenses not covered by health insurance. Unused contributions roll over to the next year. HSAs are paired with high-deductible health plans. If the HSA funds are exhausted and the deductible level has not been reached, the consumer is responsible for covering that gap. Once the consumer's spending reaches the deductible level, then coverage from the health plan takes effect. HSAs were authorized in November 2003 under the Medicare Prescription Drug, Improvement, and Modernization Act of 2003 (P.L. 108-173).[78]

Proponents of consumer-directed health care assert the merit in having people take increased responsibility for their own health care use and expenses. They predict that this approach will lead to better-informed consumers, more appropriate use of health services, and lower overall spending on health care. Opponents express concern that this approach does not recognize the possible range of health conditions in an enrolled population; and imposes a greater burden on individuals with moderate to severe health conditions. Also, opponents point out that the tax advantages of such insurance arrangements benefit the wealthy to a greater extent than those less well off.

Recent Enrollment Trends

From the mid-1990s to 2014, HMOs continued to become proportionally less popular among covered workers, declining to a 13% share of the employer-sponsored insurance market in 2014 after reaching a 31% share in 1996. For more than a decade, PPOs have made up the majority (58% share in 2014) of employer-sponsored plans—contributing to the displacement of conventional indemnity coverage, which has by now all but disappeared from the private market. PPO plans, which combine moderate provider network restrictions with increased patient freedom relative to HMOs, remain the dominant form of worker coverage today. High-deductible coverage paired with HSAs and other savings account arrangements have also made inroads in the market, making up about a fifth of employer-sponsored enrollment by 2014.[79]

The individual insurance market has seen a similar distribution of plan types. Surveys taken of health insurers show that for the individual market, just as for the group market, PPOs are the most popular option; in fact, they are overwhelmingly popular, accounting for more than 80% of self-only plans and more than 70% of family plans in 2009. In contrast, HMOs are relatively unpopular, with HMO plans declining from about 6% of self-only plans in 2004 to about 2% in 2009.[80]

End Notes

[1] Publicly funded health programs generally either provide funding for direct medical services or assist consumers in paying for health care. The latter are included in a broad category of programs based on social insurance principles. Social insurance refers to publicly funded insurance programs that are statutorily mandated for certain groups of people, such as low-income individuals.

[2] Either in terms of multiple services due to a chronic condition or a single use due to an emergency condition.

[3] While nonprofit organizations also provide health insurance in this country, such organizations nonetheless are interested in containing expenses, even if they do not have a profit motive.

[4] The premium calculation is further adjusted to reflect a variety of factors collectively known as the underwriting cycle.

[5] S. Cohen, "The Concentration and Persistence in the Level of Health Expenditures over Time: Estimates for the U.S. Population, 2011-2012," September 2014, http://meps.ahrq.gov/mepsweb/data_files/publications/st449/stat449.pdf.

[6] For additional information on the individual mandate under ACA, see CRS Report R41331, Individual Mandate Under ACA.

[7] For additional information on the ACA's insurance standards, see CRS Report R42069, Private Health Insurance Market Reforms in the Affordable Care Act (ACA).

[8] For further discussion, see "Regulation of Health Insurance."

[9] The federal tax code contains many health-related provisions that provide tax advantages to certain individuals, employers and workers, for both the purchase of health coverage and unreimbursed medical expenses. For additional information about health-related tax benefits, see Joint Committee on Taxation, "Tax Expenditures for Health Care," July 30, 2008, available at https://www.jct.gov/publications.html?func=select&id=5.

[10] 26 U.S.C. §§ 3121(a)(2), 3231(e)(1), and 3306(b)(2).

[11] U.S. Census Bureau, Current Population Survey, "Health Insurance Coverage in the United States: 2013," September 2014, available at http://www.census.gov/content/dam/Census/library/publications/2014/demo/p60-250.pdf.

[12] Congressional Budget Office, "Options for Reducing the Deficit: 2014 to 2023," November 2013, available at http://cbo.gov/sites/default/files/cbofiles/attachments/44715-OptionsForReducingDeficit-3.pdf.

[13] Debra A. Donahue, "Medical Expense Trend Up in 2011," Mark Farrah Associates, February 12, 2013, available at http://www.markfarrah.com/healthcare-business-strategy/Medical-Expense-Trend-Up-in-2011.aspx.

[14] Health Care Cost Institute, "2013 Health Care Cost and Utilization Report," October 2014, http://www.healthcostinstitute.org/files/2013%20HCCUR%2012-17-14.pdf.

[15] Debra A. Donahue, "Medical Expense Trend Up in 2011," Mark Farrah Associates, February 12, 2013, available at http://www.markfarrah.com/healthcare-business-strategy/Medical-Expense-Trend-Up-in-2011.aspx.

[16] These averages include both the employer and employee shares of the total premium. The Kaiser Family Foundation and Health Research and Educational Trust, 2014 Employer Health Benefits Survey, available online at http://files.kff.org/attachment/2014-employer-health-benefits-survey-full-report.

[17] Ibid.

[18] Jonathan Gruber, "Growth and Variability in Health Plan Premiums in the Individual Insurance Market Before the Affordable Care Act." The Commonwealth Fund. June 2014. Available at http://www.commonwealthfund.org/~/media/files/publications/issue-brief/2014/jun/1750_gruber_growth_variability_hlt_plan_premiums_ib_v2.pdf.

[19] National Association of Insurance Commissioners, "2013 Health Insurance Industry Analysis Report," available at http://www.naic.org/documents/topic_insurance_ industry_ snapshots_2013_industry_analysis_report.pdf.

[20] For additional information about ERISA, see the Department of Labor's overview document for a summary and relevant links, http://www.dol.gov/dol/topic/health-plans/erisa.htm#doltopics.

[21] For additional information about this tax deduction, see Internal Revenue Service, IRS Tax Tip 2013-43, March 28, 2013, available at http://www.irs.gov/uac/Newsroom/Dont-Miss-the-Health-Insurance-Deduction-if-Youre-SelfEmployed.

[22] For FAQs regarding HIPAA's health insurance provisions, see http://www.dol.gov/ebsa/faqs/faq_consumer_hipaa.html.

[23] For additional information on ACA provisions that affect private insurance, see CRS Report R43048, Overview of Private Health Insurance Provisions in the Patient Protection and Affordable Care Act (ACA).

[24] For additional information, see CRS Report R41331, Individual Mandate Under ACA.

[25] For additional information, see CRS Report R41159, Potential Employer Penalties Under the Patient Protection and Affordable Care Act (ACA).

[26] For additional information, see CRS Report R42069, Private Health Insurance Market Reforms in the Affordable Care Act (ACA).

[27] For additional information, see CRS Report R41137, Health Insurance Premium Credits in the Patient Protection and Affordable Care Act (ACA).

[28] For additional information, see CRS Report R41158, Summary of the Small Business Health Insurance Tax Credit Under ACA.

[29] For additional information, see CRS Report R43771, Small Business Health Options Program (SHOP) Exchange.

[30] Individuals may report more than one source of coverage, and individuals may report both private insurance and insurance through public programs; therefore, percentages presented in this report total to more than 100.

[31] Private health insurance includes employer-sponsored insurance and individual market insurance.

[32] Public programs include Medicare, Medicaid and other means-tested public programs (e.g., the State Children's Health Insurance Program, CHIP), and health care services for military service members and veterans (e.g., TRICARE).

[33] U.S. Census Bureau, Current Population Survey, "Health Insurance Coverage in the United States: 2013," September 2014, available at http://www.census.gov/content/dam/Census/library/publications/2014/demo/p60-250.pdf.

[34] U.S. Census Bureau, Current Population Survey, op. cit.

[35] Under the ACA's individual mandate, those who decline coverage from an employer and do not take up any other coverage may be subject to a penalty. For additional information, see CRS Report R41331, Individual Mandate Under ACA.

[36] The Kaiser Family Foundation and Health Research and Educational Trust, 2014 Employer Health Benefits Survey, available online at http://files.kff.org/attachment/2014-employer-health-benefits-survey-full-report.

[37] ACA's reforms to the nongroup market and establishment of exchanges and tax credits are policy levers to make the nongroup market behave more like the large group market. See the section titled "Individual Health Insurance" in this report for additional information about these issues.

[38] For additional information about this issue, see CRS Report R41159, Potential Employer Penalties Under the Patient Protection and Affordable Care Act (ACA).

[39] For additional information about small business tax credits under ACA, see CRS Report R41158, Summary of the Small Business Health Insurance Tax Credit Under ACA.

[40] Kaiser Family Foundation, "Survey of People Who Purchase Their Own Insurance," June 2010, http://kaiserfamilyfoundation.files.wordpress.com/2013/01/8077-r.pdf.

[41] U.S. Census Bureau, Current Population Survey, op. cit.

[42] For a discussion of these and other insurance market reforms in the ACA, see CRS Report R42069, Private Health Insurance Market Reforms in the Affordable Care Act (ACA).

[43] See CRS Report R41137, Health Insurance Premium Credits in the Patient Protection and Affordable Care Act (ACA).

[44] Private health insurance is primarily regulated at the state-level. The ACA establishes uniform requirements and additional options for all states.

[45] Currently, 14 states and DC have their own state-based exchanges and the remaining 36 states are participating in the Federally-facilitated Marketplace or have State Partnership Marketplaces or supported State-based Marketplaces.

[46] The 2024 projected exchange enrollment of 25 million is partially offset by a decrease of 5 million in nongroup coverage outside of the exchanges. A very small portion of this projected decrease includes other forms of coverage. Congressional Budget Office, "Updated Estimates of the Effects of the Insurance Coverage Provisions of the Affordable Care Act, April 2014," available at http://cbo.gov/sites/default/files/cbofiles/ attachments/ 45231- ACA_Estimates.pdf.

[47] U.S. Census Bureau, Current Population Survey, op. cit.

[48] U.S. Census Bureau, Current Population Survey, op. cit.

[49] For additional information about Medicare, see CRS Report R40425, Medicare Primer.

[50] U.S. Census Bureau, Current Population Survey, op. cit.

[51] For additional information about Medicaid, see CRS Report R43357, Medicaid: An Overview.

[52] For additional information about the expansion of Medicaid under ACA, see CRS Report R43564, The ACA Medicaid Expansion.

[53] For additional information about CHIP, see CRS Report R40444, State Children's Health Insurance Program (CHIP): A Brief Overview.

[54] U.S. Census Bureau, Current Population Survey, op. cit.

[55] For additional information on TRICARE and the military health system, see CRS Report RL33537, Military Medical Care: Questions and Answers.

[56] Other factors include status as a former prisoner of war or receipt of a Purple Heart.

[57] For additional information on health care for veterans and CHAMPVA, see CRS Report R42747, Health Care for Veterans: Answers to Frequently Asked Questions.

[58] U.S. Census Bureau, Current Population Survey, op. cit.

[59] Persons with income at or below 250% of the federal poverty level accounted for about 75% of all nonelderly uninsured individuals in 2012. Kaiser Family Foundation, "The Uninsured: A Primer – Key Facts about Health Insurance on the Eve of Coverage Expansions," October 2013, http://kff.org/uninsured/report/the-uninsured-a-primerkey-facts-about-health-insurance-on-the-eve-of-coverage-expansions/.

[60] Ibid., p. 17.

[61] Kaiser Commission on Medicaid and the Uninsured, "The Uninsured and the Difference Health Insurance Makes," Oct. 2011, http://www.kff.org/uninsured/upload/1420-13.pdf.

[62] Agency for Healthcare Research and Quality, "National Healthcare Disparities Report, 2013," May 2014, http://www.ahrq.gov/research/findings/nhqrdr/nhdr13/2013nhdr.pdf.

[63] There are many different types of exemptions, such as hardship, affordability, qualifying religious reasons, membership in health care sharing ministry, not lawfully present in the U.S., etc.

[64] For additional information on the individual mandate, see CRS Report R41331, Individual Mandate Under ACA.

[65] Congressional Budget Office, "Updated Estimates of the Effects of the Insurance Coverage Provisions of the Affordable Care Act, April 2014." Available at http://cbo.gov/sites/default/files/cbofiles/attachments/45231- ACA_Estimates.pdf.

[66] U.S. Census Bureau, Current Population Survey, "Health Insurance Coverage in the United States: 2013," September 2014, available at http://www.census.gov/content/dam/Census/library/publications/2014/demo/p60-250.pdf.

[67] Individuals may report more than one source of coverage, and individuals may report both private insurance and insurance through public programs; therefore percentages total to more than 100.

[68] "The Role of Prepaid Group Practice in Relieving the Medical Care Crisis," Harvard Law Review, vol. 84, no. 4 (Feb. 1971), pp. 887-1001. Available at http://www. jstor. org/stable/1339782.

[69] The Kaiser Family Foundation and Health Research and Educational Trust, 2014 Employer Health Benefits Survey, available online at http://files.kff.org/attachment/2014-employer-health-benefits-survey-full-report.

[70] Jon Gabel, et al., "Job-Based Health Benefits in 2002: Some Important Trends," Health Affairs, vol. 21, no. 5, pp. 143-151.

[71] Richard Kronick, "Waiting for Godot: Wishes and Worries in Managed Care," Journal of Health Politics, Policy and Law, vol. 24, no. 5, pp. 1099-1106.

[72] Jon Gabel et al., "Job-Based Health Insurance in 2001: Inflation Hits Double Digits, Managed Care Retreats," Health Affairs, vol. 20, no. 5, pp. 180-186.

[73] Firshein J, Sandy LG. The changing approach to managed care. In: Isaacs SL, Knickman JR, eds. To Improve Health and Health Care 2001: The Robert Wood Johnson Anthology. San Francisco: Jossey-Bass; 2001:77-100.

[74] PPOs allow plan participants and beneficiaries to use any health care provider, but offer lower cost-sharing when individuals use in-network providers, with whom the insurer has negotiated rates.

[75] The Kaiser Family Foundation and Health Research and Educational Trust, 2014 Employer Health Benefits Survey, available online at http://files.kff.org/attachment/2014-employer-health-benefits-survey-full-report.

[76] Jon B. Christianson and Sally Trude, "Managing Costs, Managing Benefits: Employer Decisions in Local Health Care Markets," Health Services Research, pt. II, vol. 38, no. 1, pp. 357-373.

[77] Jon Gabel, et al., "Job-Based Health Benefits in 2002: Some Important Trends," Health Affairs, vol. 21, no. 5, pp. 143-151.

[78] For additional information about HSAs, see CRS Report RS22877, Health Savings Accounts and High-Deductible Health Plans: A Data Primer.

[79] The Kaiser Family Foundation and Health Research and Educational Trust, 2014 Employer Health Benefits Survey, available online at http://files.kff.org/attachment/2014-employer-health-benefits-survey-full-report.

[80] America's Health Insurance Plans Center for Policy and Research, Individual Health Insurance 2009: A Comprehensive Survey of Premiums, Availability, and Benefits. Oct. 2009. Available at http://www.ahip.org/ Individual-Health-Insurance-Survey-2009/. America's Health Insurance Plans Center for Policy and Research. Individual Health Insurance: A Comprehensive Survey of Affordability, Access, and Benefits. Aug. 2005. Available at http://heartland.org/sites/all/modules/custom/heartland_migration/ files/pdfs/ 17693.pdf. Plan type information was not grouped in the same way across survey years, potentially leading to slight discrepancies between surveys. However, the broader picture illustrated by the numbers is correct.

INDEX

I

L

M

N